Matthias Claudius

Twayne's World Authors Series

Ulrich Weisstein, Editor of German Literature

Indiana University

TWAS 691

MATTHIAS CLAUDIUS
(1740–1815)
Portrait by Friederike Leisching
Courtesy of the Agricola Family, Hamburg.

Matthias Claudius

By Herbert Rowland

Eastern Washington University

Twayne Publishers • Boston

Matthias Claudius

Herbert Rowland

Published by Twayne Publishers
A Division of G. K. Hall & Company
70 Lincoln Street
Boston, Massachusetts 02111

Book Production by John Amburg

Book Design by Barbara Anderson

Printed on permanent/durable acid-free paper and bound in the United States of America.

Library of Congress Cataloging in Publication Data

Rowland, Herbert.
Matthias Claudius.

(Twayne's world authors series; TWAS 691)
Bibliography: p. 146
Includes index.
1. Claudius, Matthias, 1740–1815—Criticism and interpretation. I. Title. II. Series
PT1837.C5Z798 1983 831′.6 82-23358
ISBN 0-8057-6538-7

Contents

About the Author

Herbert Rowland, born in 1943 in Little Rock, Arkansas, studied German and English at the University of Arkansas and took the B.A. degree there. He continued his studies with the aid of scholarships and assistantships first at the University of Tübingen and then at the University of Oregon, where he received the M.A. and Ph.D. degrees. After teaching at Reedsport High School (Oregon), he went to Eastern Washington University. There, he serves as Director of German and Director of Modern Language Education and is currently an Associate Professor of German, teaching courses in German language, literature, and culture.

Professor Rowland has published articles and reviews in the United States, Canada, and Germany on Claudius and C. M. Wieland. His *Musarion and Wieland's Concept of Genre* appeared in the series *Göppinger Arbeiten zur Germanistik* in 1975.

Preface

The work of Matthias Claudius has suffered a not entirely common fate, which began to cast its spell even before the author's death in 1815. The work is read but rarely discussed. Selections and even complete editions appear perennially in the German equivalent of our *Books in Print,* typically in popular rather than scholarly format. This fact and private comments made by a number of colleagues and other individuals in the United States and Germany lead me to believe that Claudius is more alive today than many a more securely canonized German writer. And yet the professional silence is virtually palpable. The two dissertations written during the 1970s are almost as interesting for the echoes they produced in the dim and scantily furnished anteroom of Claudius scholarship as for their inherent and considerable value.[1]

The fate of Claudius's work is due in part to the Goethe-Schiller syndrome in German scholarship, the unfortunate tendency to concentrate on major figures to the neglect of the varied riches of minor writers, which only recently has been met with some determination.[2] There exists to date no historical-critical edition of the work or the correspondence worthy of the name—or the author. Claudius was indeed a minor writer, but at least since T. S. Eliot's essay on the subject there should be no shame in such an appellation.[3]

Perhaps more important is the self-evident, at times apparently unliterary quality of much of Claudius's writing. Remarks made about Robert Herrick's work in seventeenth-century England apply to the best of Claudius's production as well: "his lyrics aptly expressed and successfully communicated the meanings and emotions which he intended to convey. He thus accomplished the prime task of an artist, providing works of art which were so self-communicative that their appreciation and understanding required no explanation or commentary. . . . Such appreciation is like the appreciation due natural perfection; analysis is possible but extraneous."[4] Certainly, the power of Claudius's work to speak directly to the reader is a major reason for the longevity of its appeal, but this power has proven to be a double-edged sword.

Like Herrick, Claudius selected his themes and gave them form in personal response to specific cultural traditions and for a contemporary eighteenth-century audience. The very accessibility of his works, which has led to the assimilation of some into the anonymity of folk song, has itself concealed the conditions of his very real literary achievement and its enthusiastic reception by some of the leading personalities of the age. It has allowed other contemporaries and especially later generations to praise or condemn him for false reasons—or, as has more frequently been the case, to pass him by in benign or malevolent silence or with total indifference.

The most decisive reason for this state of affairs lies perhaps in the course of political and intellectual history since the eighteenth century. Claudius's life and work were firmly rooted in Christianity and monarchy, which both during and after his time became increasingly problematic. Claudius's own attitude toward them was highly differentiated, but his commentators have generally been less discerning. Their discussion and anthologization of certain works, usually poetry to the exclusion of prose, have frequently reflected their own orientation rather than that of the author.

Whatever the factors may be, they have united to establish a Claudius-myth fraught with contradictions. For some he is the ideal husband and father, for others a ne'er-do-well; here a literary virtuoso and wise man, there a hack and ignoramus; now a revolutionary, now a reactionary; in some circles an orthodox Lutheran, in others a Pietist or secret Catholic, and more recently an atheist in the most important moments of his life. Many have lauded and damned him for the very same thing and have, as often as not, missed the mark. Such exaggerations conceal the coherent struggle of the man and work in their own time and their possible significance for the present. Claudius, no less than Herrick, is very much in need of commentary in the twentieth century. Fortunately, the coherence of the struggle is there for all to see in his work. Claudius can be placed in both literary and intellectual history, and it is in part the task of this study to do precisely that, within the limits of a general introduction in this series.

The task is no small one, however. Claudius's work is relatively slight, to be sure, covering less than a thousand pages in the most complete edition, and its forms and themes are comparatively few.

Yet, it is comprised of some 750 individual pieces which reveal a wealth of formal variation and thematic nuance. No manageable selection can hope to do full justice to its complete range. Consequently, the study approaches his work by means of longcuts and crosscuts. The first chapter marks the stations of his life and the men and forces which shaped his experience, thought, and writing. Chapter 2 provides a summary overview of the major concerns which informed his work as theme. In Chapters 3 and 4 examples of his prose and poetry represent both the variety and continuity of his literary treatment of these concerns at various points as well as over the course of his life. The final chapter offers a brief sketch of Claudius's reception and achievement and a suggestion of his position in literature and life.

It is one of the misfortunes of literary history that Claudius has been so rarely, and then often poorly, translated into English. For if Germany ever produced a writer immediately accessible to readers beyond its borders, it was he. The universality of his central themes and the self-evident nature of their expression could speak as directly to Americans and Englishmen as they have to many Germans. The main obstacle to adequate translation is perhaps the fact that his success, especially in the lyric, is to a great extent language-specific and therefore untranslatable. Indeed, the translations used here, which are my own, seek primarily to communicate the sense rather than the literary quality of the originals and require a certain leap of faith on the part of the reader. Because of space limitations my general policy has been to present the prose only in translation. The poetry, on the other hand, appears largely in both the original and prose translation within the text. Titles, once translated, are in German.

At this point I would like to thank Eastern Washington University and the Alexander von Humboldt Foundation for providing the time and financial support for a lengthy visit in Hamburg, West Germany, where most of this book was written. I would also like to thank the librarians of Eastern Washington University, whom I plied interminably with interlibrary loan requests and who reproduced the frontispiece and the plate appearing in the book, and of Virginia Polytechnic Institute, who granted me a long-term loan of the reprint of *Der Wandsbecker Bote.* I am grateful to Ralph Bonz, Bernhard Richter, and other members of the Matthias Claudius Society and to the faculty of the Matthias Claudius Gymnasium in

Hamburg-Wandsbek for their hospitality and professional wisdom. The Agricola family graciously provided me with a copy of Friederike Leisching's portrait of Claudius for the frontispiece. I am particularly indebted to Dr. Rolf Siebke for his careful reading of the manuscript and valuable comments. Frau Anke Eck also offered useful advice on the book. She, together with Frau Heimke Maltz, neighbors, and their friends made my family's stay in Claudius's chosen hometown personally rewarding. Finally, I must express my thanks to my wife, Linda, and to our children, Stefanie and Marc, for putting up with the strains which arose from the project. I would like to dedicate the book to them and to Frau Eck and to Frau Maltz.

Herbert Rowland

Eastern Washington University

Chronology

1740	15 August: Matthias Claudius born in Reinfeld (Holstein), the son of Pastor Matthias Claudius and his second wife, Maria, née Lorck. Early instruction provided in the home.
1755	Attendance at the Latin School in Plön with older brother Josias.
1759–1762	Student of theology, later of law and public administration, at the University of Jena with Josias. Member of the German Society.
1760	Death of Josias.
1762–1764	Departure from Jena without certificate. Residence with parents in Reinfeld.
1763	*Tändeleien und Erzählungen* (second edition 1764).
1764–1765	Private secretary to Count Johann Ludwig Holstein in Copenhagen. Member of German circle around Minister Johann Hartwig Ernst von Bernstorff. Acquaintance with Friedrich Gottlieb Klopstock and Heinrich Wilhelm von Gerstenberg.
1765–1768	Residence with parents in Reinfeld. Friendship with Gottlob Friedrich Ernst Schönborn.
1768–1770	Editor of the *Adreβ-Comptoir-Nachrichten* in Hamburg. Member of circle around Hermann Samuel Reimarus. Friendship with Philipp Emanuel Bach, Gotthold Ephraim Lessing, and Johann Gottfried Herder.
1771–1775	Editor of *Der Wandsbecker Bote* in Wandsbeck, near Hamburg. Friendship with members of the *Göttinger Hain.*
1772	15 March: marriage to Rebekka Behn, who bears him twelve children. 30 September: death of first child Matthias at birth.

1774 Beginning of the correspondence with Johann Georg Hamann.

1775 Appearance of Books I and II of the collected works, *Asmus omnia sua secum portans, oder Sämtliche Werke des Wandsbecker Boten.* Trip to Berlin, friendship with Christian Graf von Haugwitz.

1776–1777 Member of *Oberlandkommission* in Darmstadt. Editor of the *Hessen-Darmstädtische privilegirte Land-Zeitung.* Serious illness, return to Wandsbeck.

1778 Book III of *Asmus.*

1783 Book IV of *Asmus.* Growing friendship with members of the Holstein nobility in and around Emkendorf.

1784 Trip to Silesia, meeting with Goethe and Wieland in Weimar and Jena.

1785 Yearly stipend granted by Danish Crown Prince Frederick.

1788 Named First Inspector of the new bank in Altona by Crown Prince Frederick. Death of son Matthias. Trip through Holstein with Friedrich Heinrich Jacobi. Beginning of appearance of significant works on theology and philosophy, politics, and art outside of *Asmus.*

1790 Book V of *Asmus.*

1793 Meeting with Princess Amalia Galizyn, closer ties with the religious circle in Münster.

1796 Death of daughter Christiane.

1798 Book VI of *Asmus.*

1803 Book VII of *Asmus.*

1804 Friendship with the young Romantic painter Philipp Otto Runge.

1810 Death of Runge. Acquaintance with several Romantic painters and poets.

1812 Book VIII of *Asmus.* Literary contact and work with Friedrich Schlegel.

1813 Beginning of nearly year-long exile with friends and relatives due to the Napoleonic Wars.

1814 8 March: return to Wandsbeck. 19 October: last public appearance at the founding of the Hamburg-Altona Bible Society. December: move to home of daughter Caroline and son-in-law Friedrich Perthes in Hamburg because of deteriorating health.

1815 21 January: Claudius dies in Hamburg and is buried in Wandsbeck.

Chapter One

An Apologia

From Country Parsonage to University (1740–1762)

Matthias Claudius was born on 15 August 1740 in Reinfeld, a village lying between Hamburg and Lübeck in Southeast Holstein.[1] His father was one in a line of seventeen Protestant pastors reaching back nearly a century and a half to the period following Luther's death. His father's earnest but conciliatory attitude toward Christianity, more Pietistic than Orthodox in color, and the two parents' openly expressed love for each other and their children, determined the tone of the personal and spiritual life of this closely knit family of twelve. Pastor Claudius himself guided his sons' education until their confirmation, instructing them not only in the classical languages and mathematics but more importantly in Christianity. The figures and stories and the language of the Bible, the melodies and rhythms of the hymnal, and the promise of salvation made by them all became integral parts of Claudius's early experience. He probably found little modern literature in his father's library; his considerable musical gifts, on the other hand, developed freely in his home environment.

Lying amid rolling, forested hills and five lakes, Reinfeld offered Claudius ample opportunity to become intimately acquainted with nature in its lovelier and more placid aspects. Retaining its small-town character even today, it also provided abundant contact and familiarity with the lives and concerns of the farmers and tradesmen of the area. The greater world was represented by a small castle nearby, where a duchess from Plön frequently gathered her family and the local gentry for visits. The pastor's family, as the educated and respected center of the community, was often in attendance, and members of the noble family served as godparents for several of the children.

Claudius's childhood passed tranquilly and fruitfully, in the main, both for his spiritual and professional development; he and his elder brother Josias were to follow in their father's footsteps. During the space of one short year, however, he saw two of his brothers and one sister pass away, and he himself once nearly drowned in the peaceful *Herrenteich* behind his home. He bore these impressions as well as many others with him, and all had a determining influence on his later experience and work.

Around 1755 Matthias and Josias set out together for the Latin School in Plön, where, aside from occasional visits with their family, they remained until 1759. At that time the regional capital of Holstein, the city afforded even closer contact with the nobility and a broader view of the world beyond the borders of their home town. With its varied lakes and forests Plön at the same time provided a familiar landscape and people as well as respite from the various challenges of school.

Here, they continued their study of Latin and Greek and, as future theologians, began to learn Hebrew as well; German and Christianity were among their other subjects. No mathematics or modern languages were offered, which led Claudius to begin even here his lifelong practice of private study. More decisive than the subject matter itself was the approach taken to it, which was dominated by the rationalistic spirit of the time. The study of literature was merely a matter of rhetoric; ancient and modern works were objects of analysis according to figures of speech and preconceived rules. Christianity was little more than a set of dogmas to be learned by rote and grasped by reason. Intellectually, Claudius certainly profited from his intensified and broadened program of instruction. Later works suggest, however, that he sensed in the literature and especially the religion taught here a lifeless but very real threat to the experience he had brought with him from Reinfeld.

In April 1759 Claudius and his brother began to study theology at the University of Jena in distant Thuringia. As a serious and capable student Claudius was predisposed to take full advantage of the opportunity provided by this center of learning and culture. He attended lectures by adherents of both the orthodox and philosophical schools represented here, and then, within a short time and unexpectedly, turned his back on both. The ostensible reason was a malady of the chest, which he felt would hinder him from performing his duties at the pulpit. However, the unyielding dogmatism of the Lutheran orthodoxy and the formalistic, half-theological and half-philosophical rationalism of the followers of Gottfried Wilhelm Leibniz and Christian Wolff may well have been contributing factors. Neither offered sustenance for his own tolerant positive Christianity or for a corresponding pastoral activity. Claudius's later religious works reveal numerous views, albeit in freer form, maintained by his orthodox teachers, and he even assimilated something of the mechanics applied to Christianity by the philosopher-theologians. Complicated perhaps by serious reservations vis-à-vis the claims of the learned, however, his physical ailment led him to decide against a calling which he could not approach wholeheartedly.

Instead, Claudius turned to the study of law and what today would be called public administration. Here, he was influenced most strongly by Johann August Schlettwein, whose utilitarian attempt to apply abstract knowledge to everyday life for the common good addressed Claudius's native pragmatism and sense of social responsibility. In time, Claudius's interests turned in another direction. However, he later expressed his gratitude to this mentor in a poem and avenged himself in other works for the intolerance and cold mental gymnastics of his other professors.[2]

The unsettling effect of Claudius's encounter with school theology was complicated in 1760. Late in the year both he and his brother fell ill with smallpox or consumption. After a long struggle Claudius recovered, only to watch helplessly as Josias suffered increasingly and finally died. The impact of his most beloved brother's death cannot be overestimated, for his attempt to understand it led first to his perhaps most severe spiritual crisis and ultimately to insights which were to see him through the many remaining trials of his life.[3]

This crisis found expression in an oration held at his brother's graveside after the fashion of the time and published late in the year under the title *Ob und wieweit Gott den Tod der Menschen bestimme* [Whether and to what extent God determines the death of men], Claudius's first appearance in print.[4] This strange mixture of academic treatise, a premature fruit of his exercises in Plön and Jena, and the most personal confession has led some of Claudius's major biographers to question his authorship.[5]

The first part of the oration represents a kind of theodicy, an attempt to vindicate God from responsibility for painful human death. In discursive language Claudius demonstrates that only the preordained, gradual disappearance of vital fluids from the body and the peaceful passing of the individual are consistent with the unquestionable view of God as a loving father. Painful death is the direct or indirect result of the individual's abuse of his own will. But at this point Claudius finds that he has reasoned himself onto the horns of an impossible dilemma. If God is not responsible for Josias's terrible death, then Josias, his loving and religiously upright brother, himself must be. And if one goes so far as to suppose that God is responsible for all human events, as some suggest, then how can such a death possibly further the perfection of the unseen whole? Here, Claudius asks Voltaire's question posed in the face of the appallingly destructive earthquake in Lisbon in 1755. Claudius cannot draw the logical conclusion from his argumentation and has no answer to his question. As if silently acknowledging his untenable position, he ends the demonstration abruptly, ceases his questioning, and gives instead a heart-rending description of his brother's torment and his own helplessness, ending with the desperate declaration of faith, "No, *God,* no, you did not determine his death. I am unhappy, but you are innocent . . . it was not your will."[6]

Claudius left his brother's grave with his faith sorely tested but intact, perhaps strengthened, and with a deeper sense of the mystery of life and death. He continued his studies less with doubt in God than in the capacity of human reason to penetrate this mystery, "mere reason, which is too nearsighted to see all the principles according to which *God* acts."[7] He never again sought to lift the veil of this and other mysteries in such a manner, but the complex of life, death, faith, and human reason remained his central concern for the rest of his life.

Claudius's waning interest in his professional studies was soon compensated by an enthusiasm for literature. He early became a member of the *Teutsche Gesellschaft* ("German Society") at the university, an organization of professors and students devoted to the study and improvement of German language and literature. Their own scholarly and literary products remained largely insignificant and tradition-bound. Nominally, however, they sought to free themselves from the normative-systematic poetics of French Classicism as represented by Johann Christoph Gottsched and the Leipzig School and to approach the less restrained and less rationalistic position of the Swiss theoreticians Johann Jakob Bodmer and Johann Jakob Breitinger, schooled on English literature. During Saturday-afternoon meetings among like-minded young men Claudius became familiar with the figures and forms of contemporary German literature. He also met two of the leaders of the nascent literary avant-garde. Jakob Friedrich Schmidt, remembered now as a minor critic, served as Claudius's literary mentor, commenting on his own work and helping him to understand that of Friedrich Gottlieb Klopstock. He also mediated Claudius's friendship with Heinrich Wilhelm von Gerstenberg, whose *Tändeleien und Erzählungen* [Trifles and tales] of 1759 had already earned him a reputation and whose later literary and critical work made him a major figure in the early *Sturm und Drang* ("storm and stress") movement.

The stimulation which Claudius received from the society found expression in his own *Tändeleien und Erzählungen,* published in 1763 after his departure from Jena. Contemporary and subsequent critics have been unanimous in their condemnation of this imitation of Gerstenberg. Indeed, today's reader is likely to find little in the often clumsy dallying of Claudius's Rococo shepherds and shepherdesses or in the wooden, sentimental moralizing of his verse narratives to attract him or to remind him of the later poet. Claudius included only one of the poems in his collected works.[8] However, the need for a second edition the very next year indicates that the work was not without readers. Claudius continued to write in this vein, if infrequently, even after he had found his more characteristic manner. The bucolic figures and landscape of the work live on in the innocent youths and maidens and the goddess Selena of his romantic reverie and, transformed by maturity, in the farmers of the later works as well. A few pieces still warrant passing attention as signs of his current emotional experience and intellectual direction as well as of his developing aesthetic sensibility.[9] And his experiments with the narratives—for such both the tales and poems were—played a modest role in the formation of his prose style.

Sometime during 1762 Claudius left Jena without officially finishing his studies and returned to Reinfeld. The three years he had spent in Jena completed the foundation of what became an admirable store of learning and pointed out the direction, however vaguely for the moment, which his professional life was to take. Moreover, the experiences which they brought provided greater clarity in his attitude toward the role of learning and vocation in his life and toward his spiritual-worldly inheritance from Reinfeld. However, it would take years to assimilate these experiences and place them in the proper perspective, for the impressions of his lectures and his brother's death were still fresh in his mind. Without a leaving certificate, his first literary effort decimated by the critics, he had no clear-cut path before him. His mood remained dark for some time to come.

Asmus's Apprenticeship and Early Journeywork (1762–1775)

Little is known of Claudius's life during the two years he spent in Reinfeld after returning from the university. Some of his biographers, apparently motivated by the Protestant work ethic, have paused at this juncture to comment with more or less good will on a certain *vis inertiae* in his character, which prevented him, now as later, from enjoying the blessings of regular employment.[10] Indeed, some of his contemporaries accused him of outright laziness. There is perhaps a grain of truth in these views, but other explanations can be offered as well for the irregular turns in his professional life. It can be said at this point that Claudius was loath to pursue any activity, such as the ministry, which could not claim his whole being and that the prevalent economic and social conditions in Germany did not provide well for the free scholarly and literary existence of later times which was most congenial to his nature and which he indeed lived in his own way.[11]

In any event, the six letters to Gerstenberg which remain of the correspondence of this period attest to Claudius's serious, if unsuccessful, attempts to find a position. They also reveal a wide range of moods, fluctuating from despair to humorous acceptance of his lot. Claudius had simply not yet come to terms with the recent past. Having been so ill-received by the literary world, he limited his writing to two negligible and unpublished poems.[12] The significance of the interlude in his father's home may well lie in a psychological regrouping of forces.

However, Claudius's time in Reinfeld was not entirely uneventful for his literary and intellectual growth. He soon became close friends with Gottlob Friedrich Ernst Schönborn, tutor in a nearby village and later career diplomat. Claudius found in him a more experienced, kindred spirit, whose wide range of interests and knowledge broadened his own horizons. Schönborn is likely to have provided Claudius with his first insights into the work of Shakespeare, who was to become the hero of the younger generation in its attempt to escape the confines of Gottsched's school. He may also have introduced his friend to the emotive language of Pindar and furthered his acquaintance with Klopstock. Equally significant, Schönborn shared Claudius's interest in mathematics, and together the two studied the works of Descartes, Newton, and Bacon, who was to figure importantly in Claudius's later thought and writing.

Apparently through the mediation of his uncle, Josias Lorck, pastor at the German church in Christianshavn, Claudius eventually received a position as secretary to Count Johann Ludwig Holstein, an adviser to the Danish crown, and in March of 1764 he left Reinfeld for Copenhagen.[13] His stay there was not long, for little more than a year later he tendered his resignation and returned home. Neither the work nor the supercilious treatment accorded to him by his superior had any appeal for him. Yet, his brief visit in the Danish capital, then capital of his native Holstein as well, brought him still a step closer to the center of contemporary cultural life.

Copenhagen during this period has been called the most important precursor of the Weimar of the following decades.[14] While Frederick V may have been "the Great" in name rather than in deed, he had the good sense to surround himself for the most part with men of unquestioned ability and good will. Chief among these was Count Johann Hartwig Ernst von Bernstorff, his foreign minister and first adviser. Deeply religious, familiar with the personalities and works of recent literature and philosophy, and widely experienced in political affairs, Bernstorff sought to guide Denmark's foreign and internal policy in the best sense of enlightened absolutism. He also attempted to establish Copenhagen as the cultural and political heart of Northern Europe. By the time of Claudius's arrival he had already assembled an imposing roundtable of Germany's literary elite, which numbered among its members Klopstock and Gerstenberg.

Claudius was given a warm welcome by his countrymen and soon made fast friendships, notably with Gerstenberg, whom he now came to know personally, and Klopstock. They learned to value his basic earnestness and sparing but pertinent contributions to table conversation and, most of all, his unpretentiousness and good humor. For Claudius's mood seems to have brightened considerably over the past months. He participated vigorously in the group's favorite pastime, ice-skating, and even offered competition to Klopstock, who is said to have dedicated his ode "Der Eislauf" [Ice-skating] to Claudius's feats on the frozen lakes of the area.[15] Claudius, in turn, shared their respect for Bernstorff's benevolent leadership, their religiosity, and their artistic sympathies as well.

The Copenhagen circle was an early focal point of Germany's creative response to the sociopolitical and cultural developments of the century both at home and abroad. The characteristic ideals of the 1770s—nature, genius, creativity, feeling, freedom, and humanity—were anticipated, if not clearly conceived and formulated, here. And all emerged from the context of Germany's strong religious tradition, political provincialism, and cultural dependence. The German enlightenment was never as antireligious and anticlerical as the French; political fragmentation militated against revolutionary realization of ideals, and the absence of a definite cultural identity led to a receptivity for native and foreign influences perceived as congenial.

Consequently, Klopstock placed his own creative genius in the service of religion, seeing in his poetry a mission destined to uplift the souls of his fellow men and to evoke an emotional revelation of divine truth. In his *Der Messias* [The Messiah] and numerous odes he fashioned a flexible poetic language capable of modulating rhythm to accommodate feelings of varying intensity. He recommended Homer, Milton, and Ossian as well as Shakespeare as models of natural, intuitive art and pointed through word and deed to the Bible and Germanic history and myth as sources for the rejuvenation of a distinctly German literature, thus preparing the way for the development of a cultural patriotism which soon spread far beyond Copenhagen. Gerstenberg quickly turned Klopstock's inspiration and his own reflections to advantage. Shortly after Claudius's departure he published his "Gedicht eines Skalden" [Poem of a skald] (1766), the earliest German imitation of Ossian, and began to bring out his *Briefe über die Merkwürdigkeiten der Literatur* [Letters about the peculiarities of literature] (1766–1771); in 1768 he released his lyrical tragedy *Ugolino.*

Claudius apparently did not write a single line of verse or word of prose during his year in Copenhagen. He surely participated in the discussions of his friends with understanding and increasing insight and perhaps had a close look at Gerstenberg's workshop. Certainly, he took more than he gave. However, it is difficult to judge the extent to which he received a truly formative influence, for his own character and sensibility were rapidly assuming sharper contour and his self-confidence was growing. He wrote a highly revealing, positive review of Klopstock's odes in 1771 but eventually took a skeptical position toward the Bardic movement and the patriotic fervor of his friends. The marked critical independence of his maturity probably has its origin even in this early period. In any case the pleasure and stimulation of the company in Copenhagen could not compensate for his dissatisfaction with his position and his superior, and by the summer of 1765 he was once again in Reinfeld.

Less is known of the next three years of Claudius's life than of any other period. The question of profession occupied him, for he disliked burdening his father financially. However, he seems to have worried little about his plight. His reports to Schönborn on the daily this and that already reveal the unsentimental humor for which he eventually became famous. This lengthy stay in Reinfeld, much like the earlier, briefer one, may have served to complete his maturation. Whatever the case, the Claudius who wrote "An —— als ihm die —— starb" [To —— On the Death of His ——] perhaps as early as 1766 and entered public view again two years later in Hamburg is, in all essentials, the Claudius who is known today.[16]

While the Hanseatic League had lost its remaining claims to glory during the Thirty Years' War, Hamburg had since attained a position of political independence and commercial prominence. Even more than Copenhagen, it represented by the 1760s the economic center of and gateway to Northern Germany and Europe. Open not only to the mercantile influence of England, the river city became the scene of some of the most important religious and cultural controversies of the time. The failure of the national theater and the nickname "Stomachopolis" suggest something of Hamburg's resistance to high culture. Nevertheless, the poets Paul Fleming, Barthold Hinrich Brockes, and Friedrich von Hagedorn had found a home there, and even now an intellectual and artistic elite strove to make headway against the recalcitrance of the time and place.

The focal point of this elite was the house of the theologian and philosopher Hermann Samuel Reimarus, where, as in the homes of Bernstorff and Klopstock in Copenhagen, men of various professions and kindred persuasion met for entertainment and discussion. Together with members of his family, Reimarus coupled criticism of orthodox belief in biblical revelation, based on English Deism, with earnest philanthropic activity. Julius Gustav Alberti represented a similar, more philosophical and tolerant attitude toward Christianity, both at table and from the pulpit of St. Catherine's, where the orthodox senior pastor, Johann Melchior Goeze, was soon to mount his campaign against these and other "heretical" views. The more world-oriented members of the group maintained utilitarian ideals resembling those of Claudius's professor Schlettwein in Jena.

Around the time of Claudius's arrival three new individuals enriched the circle with their presence. In 1767 Carl Philipp Emanuel Bach, a son of Johann Sebastian, moved to Hamburg to continue his efforts to counter the influence of light Italian music with his own more serious work and that of Handel and Gluck. Gotthold Ephraim Lessing, already Germany's foremost culture and literary critic and its leading dramatist, arrived during the same year to help establish the ill-fated national theater. And in 1770 Johann Gottfried Herder appeared, who, following the lead of his mentor Johann Georg Hamann, soon went far beyond Gerstenberg to become, with Schiller, the major theorist of the last quarter of the century in Germany.

As in Copenhagen, Claudius was received warmly by the circle in Hamburg and formed several lifelong friendships, most importantly perhaps with Herder. In his new position he responded to the personalities and concerns of these as well as other individuals. Over the next few years he became increasingly aware of his spiritual kinship to Hamann, for example, which is reflected in both the content and style of certain works written during this time.[17] However, his response to the "Magus of the North" and all others was that of an essentially complete, distinctive personality.[18] As he now entered upon his period of most active participation in the mainstream of cultural life, his writing revealed a self-conscious separation of the congenial from the incompatible.

A prominent relative of Klopstock, Polykarp August Leisching, brought about this fortunate, if temporary, change in Claudius's financial and professional situation. Leisching had recently gained the royal concession to publish two new newspapers in the city, the *Hamburgische Neue Zeitung* [New Hamburg newspaper] and a regular supplement with the title *Adreβ-Comptoir-Nachrichten* [Registry office news]. He invited Claudius initially to assist in the editing of both papers but in a short time gave him sole responsibility for the supplement. Unlike its parent organ, the *Adreβ-Comptoir-Nachrichten* was to be limited to matters of interest primarily to local merchants—announcements of arrivals and departures of ships, weather reports, news from the exchange, and the like. However, Claudius sought to enliven even this banal material with humorous commentary and, following his own main interest, gradually developed a modest feuilleton with an original accent.

The moral weeklies made famous in Europe early in the century by the Englishmen Joseph Addison and Sir Richard Steele had by now long since begun their decline.[19] However, their formal influence was still apparent even in periodicals with divergent thematic orientation. Claudius paid tribute to this tradition by presenting his independent contributions to the paper in the guise of fictitious correspondents. He also employed the forms of his models, the fictional dialogue and correspondence and the treatise, which were now standard literary as well as journalistic fare.

Claudius broached a wide variety of subjects in the paper, ranging from contemporary manners and morality to literature, from philosophy and religion to natural science. His tone modulated from the discursive to the reflective and from the whimsical to the riotously satirical. Even in his lightest moments, however, he disclosed a will to edify as well as to amuse his readers. The significance of his work for the newspaper lies not only in his experimental adoption of journalistic forms and in the development of a characteristic prose style. Some of the works are little masterpieces, revealing a surprising coherence of artistic intent and execution, an *aesthetica in nuce* and a philosophy of knowledge. Claudius's unexpected maturity is evident in some of the verse as well.

The last letter to the reader was written in October 1770, little more than two years after the first. The reasons for Claudius's leaving his position are not clear; however, a letter to Schönborn suggests that he and Leisching had had a disagreement which had led to a sharp reprimand from his superior.[20] Claudius was in any case little disposed to take the affront sitting down. Closing his eyes to the debts which had mounted due to poor pay and despite all frugality, he once again chose the uncertainty of independence. Two weeks after the letter of farewell, however, he was already able to write to Gerstenberg of new prospects.[21]

In 1762 Count Heinrich Carl von Schimmelmann had bought the country estate of Wandsbeck, situated an hour by foot from Hamburg off the main road to Lübeck and near a small market town bearing its name. Wandsbeck was then the home of a newspaper which had for years regaled its primarily uncultivated readers with the latest scandals among the wealthy and powerful of Hamburg. In response to the complaints of officials in the city Schimmelmann brought publication of the paper to a halt and sought a publisher for a new organ which would raise the level of knowledge and taste in the community. He succeeded in stirring the interest of Johann Joachim Bode, an active publisher and translator and an associate of Lessing in his enterprises in Hamburg. Already familiar with Claudius and his work, Bode offered him the editorship of the new undertaking.

Der Wandsbecker Bote [The Wandsbeck messenger] made its first appearance on New Year's Day, 1771. Claudius's view of its mission is evident in his design for the heading: an owl and a youth playing a flute sit atop the title vignette, looking down on four frogs croaking below—symbols of wisdom, art, and humor. Despite the ambitious heading its impression was unimposing enough. Composed of two quarto sheets of poor-quality blotting paper, the newspaper four times weekly offered three pages of news and one of feuilleton, much like the *Hamburgische Neue Zeitung* and many other papers of the time.

Claudius had to spend an inordinate amount of time reading and sifting other papers for newsworthy events from the world at large—a common practice of the day—and then spicing his reports with anecdotes and ironic barbs to make them more attractive. Eventually, articles by personal contacts in Copenhagen, Lisbon, and even Algiers eased this burden somewhat and added an unusual note to the paper. At the outset he even had difficulty in finding contributors for the feuilleton. Over the next four and a half years, however, he was able to include poems by some of the most famous writers of both the older and younger generations, from the Anacreontics and Rationalists to representatives of the *Sturm und Drang*, which reached its highpoint during these years.[22] In all probability it was many of these as well as less familiar writers and scholars who filled the *Gelehrte Sachen* [Learned matters] of the paper with largely unsigned articles on all manner of current subjects. The fame of Claudius's enterprise gradually spread through cultural circles all over the country. Johann Heinrich Voβ, a member of the youthful group of Klopstock admirers, the *Göttinger Hain*, represented the view of many when he called *Der Wandsbecker Bote* one of the two most readable papers in Germany.[23]

Again drawing on the tradition of the moral weeklies and his experience in Hamburg, Claudius in the very first number assumes the guise of the Wandsbeck Messenger himself. Calling himself "a messenger and nothing more," the persona presents the contents of his pouch—and the program of the paper—in doggerel verses which have a comically helpless effect.[24] Behind this simplicity, however, lies a personality with a keen wit and common-sense intelligence, a love of human warmth, spontaneity, and truth in all forms as well as a broad range of knowledge and interests. Claudius soon created two companions for Asmus, as the messenger is soon called.[25] His *Vetter* ("cousin") represents a more learned variation on the messenger, with whom Asmus can speak, correspond, and travel as the occasion requires. Andres, the silent recipient of numerous letters over the following years, has the heart but not the mind of his two friends. Asmus, *Vetter,* and Andres are essentially alter egos of each other and of Claudius himself.[26] Together, they form the basis of a fictitious circle of relatives, friends, and acquaintances which over the years came to include many members.

Through the personalities of his personae Claudius approaches the most varied subjects of both topical and general interest in his prose. Humorous criticism of formalistic philosophy appears side by side with reflections on the beauty of nature, a brief history of music, and thoughts on the political system. Claudius devoted considerable space to reviews of the newest publications on the book market, in which major and minor authors come under close scrutiny and receive surprisingly perceptive appraisal. While Claudius judges primarily the man perceived in the work rather than the work itself, friendship is no guarantee against criticism. He cannot find enough words of praise for Klopstock's odes, yet he remains cool toward *Die deutsche Gelehrten-Republique* [The German republic of scholars].[27] His generally enthusiastic reception of Herder's works of this period is tempered by questioning of significant details.[28] On the other hand, he has a sense of the uniqueness and virtuosity of Goethe's *Die Leiden des jungen Werthers* [The sorrows of young Werther] and Christoph Martin Wieland's *Der neue Amadis* [The new Amadis], works which he basically rejects.[29] In the many reviews and the pieces on genius found in these pages, desultory as they may appear, the poetics which took shape in the *Adreß-Comptoir-Nachrichten* assumed even sharper focus.

Expressions of religious experience and responses to theological questions form the content of numerous feuilletons, which should give pause to those who register surprise at the emphasis placed on religion and Christianity in the later works.[30] Indeed, *Eine Disputation* [A disputation], which was published separately in 1772, contains in a nutshell the essence of Claudius's religion. His poetic contributions to the paper reveal a considerably widened range of themes and forms. While the specifically lyric production is rather small, it contains all the same a few of his most popular and best pieces, such as "Die Mutter bei der Wiege" [The mother by the cradle].

The appearance of a masterful poem on motherly love during this time is not fortuitous. On moving to Wandsbeck late in 1770, Claudius had met Rebekka Behn, the sixteen-year-old daughter of a local master joiner, and soon fallen in love with her. They became engaged in September of the next year, and Claudius could scarcely contain his joy over his "farm girl" in the announcements to Gerstenberg and Herder which followed.[31] On the evening of 15 March 1772, Claudius invited Klopstock, Bode, Schönborn, the local pastor, and a few other friends to his home, where he and Rebekka were to entertain them. Sometime during the evening he began to talk about getting married in a joking way. He then suddenly pulled a marriage license and guide from a bag, and the ceremony took place right on the spot—one of many examples of Claudius's roguishness and spontaneity.[32]

The circumstances of Claudius's first acquaintance with Rebekka and their long life together gradually assumed legendary proportions, not entirely free of contradiction and sentimentality.[33] It seems certain, however, that theirs was an unusually happy marriage, firmly grounded in mutual love and respect within the traditional relationship between husband and wife. Rebekka combined physical beauty and unpretentious charm with earnest religiosity and peace of mind. While an "insignificant farm girl" perhaps in the beginning, she possessed a flexibility of mind which enabled her to learn from her husband and his friends and to move easily in highly cultivated bourgeois and noble circles. She willingly and lovingly raised ten of twelve children to maturity, thus allowing her "Matz" to devote much of his time to study and writing.

Claudius, in turn, cared for his "Bebelmus" ("frightened mouse") tenderly during and after her pregnancies and gladly attended to the various needs of the children and day-to-day life. He spent many hours simply playing with them, himself in many respects still a child at heart, and exercised much of his inventiveness in devising new games and regular family festivals. As the children grew older, there were family concerts as well. Indeed, Claudius thrived on his family life and has been called in well-meant exaggeration a father by profession.[34] In later years, due to the vicissitudes of the times and age—he was fifty-four when his last child was born—he increasingly relinquished responsibility for the daily care and education of the children. In both conversation and writing, however, he was a source of spiritual and practical guidance and remained for both family and most friends the model husband and father. His family responded by restoring the inner stability which he had lacked since Reinfeld and was to require in later life. It furnished confirmation of his view of the relationship between God and man and a conviction which he could carry from the private sphere into the public.

The beginnings of an alleged idyllic existence fall, according to some commentators, in these first five years in Wandsbeck, and external circumstances tend to lend credence to the misapprehension.[35] After all, Wandsbeck was a rural area despite its proximity to Hamburg; indeed, citizens of the city sought refuge from metropolitan life on weekend strolls through the peaceful Wandsbeck Wood. Claudius himself kept farm animals in the small yard behind his rented house on the Steindamm and spent hours listening to nightingales or drinking tea and smoking a pipe with his friends. His older friendships and growing fame created a constant stream of visitors. Through Klopstock he met members of the *Göttinger Hain* and closed a long friendship with Voβ. With a number of his friends he joined a lodge of the Free Masons in Hamburg, whose activities reflected the humanitarian concerns of the age. Through Herder he began correspondences with Hamann and the Anacreontic poet Ludwig Gleim. And Johann Kaspar Lavater, the famous Swiss writer and physiognomist, himself initiated an exchange of letters with the Messenger of Wandsbeck. Claudius was at the deepest point of his immersion in the cultural mainstream and beyond that joyously married. His letters during the period are the most humorous and exuberant he ever wrote.[36]

Even in his engagement announcements to Gerstenberg and Herder, however, Claudius had asked for help in locating a new position, for he recognized that his income from the paper would not long support a family. Out of the impatience of love and simple faith—or, as some friends had it, out of foolhardiness—he had proceeded with his plans to marry. Claudius possessed an admirable ability to face privation with a smile. Still, this did not prevent him from trying to correct fortune himself, even if it meant leaving Wandsbeck—all the more so as subscriptions to the newspaper failed to meet hopes and expectations from the very outset. The effervescent wit of the letters beginning around 1772 is frequently accompanied by requests for aid in finding the elusive congenial job—and Claudius rarely wrote of his innermost concerns.

Bode sought to appeal to a broader audience by changing the name of the paper in 1773 to *Der Deutsche, sonst Wandsbecker Bote* [The German, formerly Wandsbeck messenger]. However, neither this step nor the success of the paper among cultivated readers had the desired result. Increasingly aware of the futility of his efforts, Claudius eventually lost interest in the endeavor, which led to unpleasantness with Bode and by June 1775 to his dismissal. A few months later publication ceased. Thus, *Der Wandsbecker Bote* shared the fate of most other contemporary papers. In the meantime it had lived a comparatively long life and moreover left its mark on Claudius and German literature as well.[37]

Despite the activity and acclaim, the pleasant surroundings, friends, and marriage, the early days in Wandsbeck had not all been bright. Claudius and Rebekka had been forced to live from hand to mouth, and the specter of death had risen before them twice: their first child, Matthias, had died at birth in 1772 and Pastor Claudius the following year. The birth of their second child, Caroline, in 1774 could not entirely erase the pain and brought moreover an additional financial concern. With the fortunes of the paper steadily declining, Claudius once again found himself facing a familiar situation. As early as 1771 he had considered the possibility of collecting his contributions to the *Adreß-Comptoir-Nachrichten* and *Der Wandsbecker Bote* for separate publication.[38] Now, in October 1774, he seriously set about executing the plan.

A New Journey (1775–1777)

At the Easter book fair in Hamburg in 1775 a slender volume appeared under the unusual title *Asmus omnia sua secum portans, oder Sämtliche Werke des Wandsbecker Boten, I. und II. Teil* [Asmus carrying

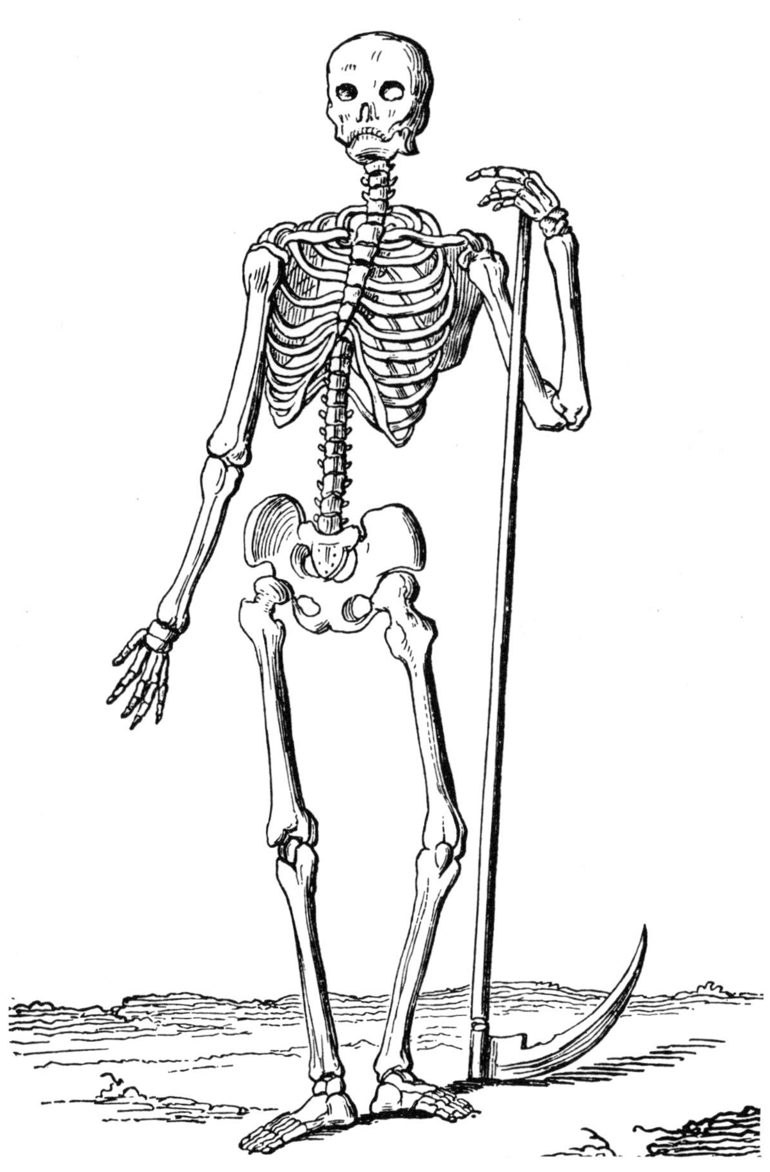

Freund Hain

all his things, or collected works of the Wandsbeck messenger, Parts I and II]. Even more striking than the title page were those which preceded and followed it. The frontispiece depicts the Grim Reaper leaning on his scythe, the name *Freund Hain* ("Friend Hain") inscribed below, and is explained a few pages later in the words, "The *first* plate . . . is *Freund Hain.* I dedicate my book to him, and *he* will stand as patron saint and household god at the front door of the book."[39] The dedication proper is directed to *Freund Hain* himself:

> They say there're people, call'm great minds, that don't pay any attention to *Hain* their whole lives long and even make fun of him and his skinny legs behind his back. I'm not a great mind. To tell the truth, I get cold chills up and down my back every time I look at you. And still I'd like to think that you're a *good* man if a person gets to know you well enough; still I feel as if I was some way homesick for you and brave enough to face you, you old Ruprecht Pförtner, that you'll come one day *to ease my hunger* and lay me safely to rest *at the right spot* to wait for better times.
>
> I've written a little book here and want to give it to you now. They're poems and prose. Don't know if you like poems, doubt it though, since you're not much at all for trifles, and they say the times are gone when poems were anything more. I hope some of the things in the book won't completely displease you. Most of it's trimming and child's play, do what you want to with it.
>
> Let me shake your hand, *Hain,* and whenever you come don't be hard on me and my friends.[40]

As if taking a deep breath, looking into the past and future and placing both in the proper perspective, Claudius once again slipped into the figure of Asmus and set out on an even more significant journey.

Six more volumes were to appear over the next thirty-seven years, all bearing the same title and all renewing the same dedication either directly or indirectly. During this period the mosaic which had begun to develop in the newspapers continued to take shape under Claudius's hand. It drew its substance from the material of his personal experience—a primary awareness of spiritual life and physical death compounded organically with religion, nature, family, the intellectual disciplines, and art. In its variegation it reflects all the tints and shades of this experience, its exuberant joy and abject sorrow and all the gradations in between. Indeed, Claudius's work and life were to a remarkable degree identical. The poet Friedrich von Matthisson, one of a number of contemporaries who knew of this identity, once wrote, "Claudius is one of the few distinguished mortals in the German Republic of Scholars in whom man and writer are the same person and in whom one can grow as fond of the one as of the other."[41] And Claudius himself once wrote, "Didn't you tell me yourself I should write in my way? And I don't care to demonstrate any distinction between writer and man, and my writing is reality with me, or at least should be, otherwise the devil take it."[42]

It was his existence in all its fullness and frailty, a life lived in constant tension with its end and the beyond, which Claudius in the figure of a lone messenger carried along with him and dedicated to the figure of death. As the humorous and familiar tone of address to *Freund Hain* suggests, Claudius rarely betrays the morbidity and pathos of the seventeenth century's encounter with life and death. He was able to live and express the joy of the moment like few others. However, he experienced both joy and sorrow in the full awareness of *Hain*'s uncanny presence and final implacability. Toward the end of Book VII, which was intended to be the last, a farewell to the reader includes the words, "I *had* to do what's right and what I promised the *friend referred to* in the 'Dedication' in the very *first part.* He'll be coming soon, and I mustn't get on the wrong side of him."[43] At least from the appearance of Books I and II of the collected works Claudius perceived and presented his life and work ultimately as a justification or *apologia pro vita sua,* before himself, his fellow men, and the God he believed in despite all trials of faith.

The volume which came out in 1775 contained a selection primarily of Claudius's already familiar work. Somewhat less than half of his contributions to *Der Wandsbecker Bote* appeared together with a number of the best pieces first published in other organs or separately; only three works were entirely new. These ninety-four pieces, spread over a mere 232 pages and varying greatly in theme and form, create the same scattered impressions today as they did then. However, careful consideration of the new order of appearance and formal changes of numerous pieces reveals a self-conscious technique of composition and arrangement which characterizes the later volumes as well.

The critical response to *Asmus I–II* was in the main very positive.[44] Claudius's friends and even Goethe and Wieland helped spread the news of its publication, and the financial returns proved sufficient to keep Claudius's head above water for a time, despite the appearance of a pirated edition. In the long run, however, the book was little more than a stopgap measure, and a period of renewed insecurity ensued, complicated by the birth of Claudius's second daughter, Christiane. Various plans were discussed; trips to Reinfeld and Lübeck were made; friends and acquaintances put out feelers all over Germany and Switzerland—all to no avail. Claudius traveled secretively to Berlin during the year, apparently in connection with his activity as a Mason. Here, he met Baron Christian von Haugwitz, who played a prominent role in later years. On his return to Wandsbeck with the *Hain*-poets Christian and Friedrich Leopold von Stolberg, however, his prospects were no brighter than before.

It was Herder who finally rescued Claudius from his predicament. In contact with prominent circles in Darmstadt through his marriage, he succeeded in securing the interest of Baron Friedrich Karl von Moser, the first minister of Hesse-Darmstadt, for his friend. From the beginning there was uncertainty on both sides regarding the exact nature of Claudius's future duties. Was he to become private tutor to the crown prince, member of an agricultural commission to be formed, or warden of a secluded castle? For Claudius, the question remained unanswered through the summer and autumn of 1775. He would have preferred the latter possibility, for he had grown deeply attached to rural Wandsbeck and remembered all too well his year at court in Copenhagen. However, necessity dictated acceptance of the official notification of his well-paid appointment to the *Oberlandkommission.* In March 1776, full of reservations but determined to give his position his best and prepared for an indefinite stay, he sold most of his belongings in Wandsbeck and headed south.

Moser had earned fame and respect throughout Germany with his works on politics, in which he paid homage to the ideals of Bernstorff and other enlightened statesmen and philosophers. The *Oberlandkommission,* which was to direct a broad program aimed at material and intellectual improvement of the largely rural land, represented his attempt to realize these ideals within his own sphere of practical influence. In view of his own origins and inclinations Claudius could only heartily approve of such a project. However, the way from theory to practice proved to be long and frequently obstructed. Claudius's letters reveal little of his daily business contacts and activity, which probably consisted mainly of paper work. Yet, it soon became apparent that the thin air in Darmstadt, of which he complained continually, was not the only source of his early dissatisfaction. In a letter to Herder in August he wrote that his work was not what his friend imagined and that he had had differences with his immediate superior, the Finance Councillor Carl Valentin Eymes.[45] He also spoke to Moser in this regard, who then sought to find more congenial and yet purposeful work for him.

In addition to his main position on the commission Claudius had, all along, served as an officer of the Invaliden-und Soldaten-Waisen-Anstalt, an institution responsible for the care of disabled soldiers and orphans. Now, at Moser's bidding, he became editor of the *Hessen-Darmstädtische privilegirte Land-Zeitung* [Hesse-Darmstadt privileged country newspaper], published by the institution and devoted to the goals of the commission.[46] Behind the mask of the old lame veteran Görgel—Asmus with more limited horizons—Claudius filled the customary political section with news from abroad, especially reports on the progress of the American Revolution. In the remaining pages he included accounts of events from all over the land, detailed information on improvements in farm management, and announcements of governmental reforms. In keeping with his social responsibility he dispensed with the feuilleton and integrated even his fictional contributions into the general program of the paper.

Claudius edited the paper, despite its immediate success, for little more than two short months. He simply never succeeded in gaining a foothold in Darmstadt. For all the natural beauty of the area, which is said to have provided the experience behind his most famous poem, "Abendlied" [Evening song], the climate disagreed with the whole family and apparently contributed to a constant sickliness.[47] Members of the governmental and cultural circles in Darmstadt made every effort to make him feel at home. While he respected Moser, the critic Johann Heinrich Merck, and a number of other new acquaintances, however, he failed to meet sympathetic spirits comparable to his friends in Hamburg and Wandsbeck. The diversion of the famous theater in Mannheim, the occasional visit of a Lessing, and his continued correspondence could not compensate for the daily contact he had thrived on earlier. He and Rebekka suffered in part from pure homesickness.

Moreover, Claudius's relationship with Eymes continued to deteriorate, which diminished his already minimal interest in what had proven to be his daily routine. The councillor treated him in an unbearably condescending manner and proceeded disreputably in a suit against a man whom Claudius considered highly respectable. If such an individual and, beyond that, representative of a benevolent government could be considered humane and noble, then Claudius understood nothing of the matter and refused to be called humane and noble himself.[48] Eymes was evidently not the only questionable personality in high position. The visibly flawed implementation of Moser's grand program and the resultant futility of his own endeavors despite his best intentions and efforts sapped his physical and emotional strength. The solution was obvious and not unfamiliar. However, the embarrassment of failure, even in view of the extenuating circumstances, stood in the way of resignation. Then there was Herder to consider, who would be disappointed, angry, and, worse yet, compromised. And where was the money to come from to put food on the table for the again expectant Rebekka and their two children? The cumulative effect of his experiences in Darmstadt was devastating.

A letter from Moser late in February made the decision easier.[49] In a generally polite if somewhat condescending tone the minister noted Claudius's obvious disenchantment with the commission and the need to replace him as well as Claudius's "inappropriate" and "misinformed" remarks on the program and its representatives. He then offered Claudius the option of continuing his work for the newspaper at least until the end of the year or handing in his resignation within six weeks. After a few days of thought Claudius calmly composed the reasons for his disappointment and comments and resigned, referring to the fact that he had come to act, not to write, honestly and beautifully.[50]

Some years later a major scandal centering around the commission broke out. Accusations of widespread inefficiency and corruption among the highest officials flew, trials ensued, numerous individuals, including Moser himself, were removed from office, and some, Eymes among them, were even imprisoned. In a written self-defense Moser remarked sarcastically on Claudius's "laziness" and inability to adjust to life in Darmstadt but was still objective enough to attribute the success of the newspaper to him.[51] Evidence gathered in part by Merck against Moser and the others sought to vindicate

Claudius's public and private conduct.[52] While probably neither quite as white or black as painted by the opposing parties, Claudius could later look back on the affair with a certain amount of satisfaction.

In early March 1777, however, completely exhausted by the ordeal, Claudius became ill with pleurisy and hovered close to death for several days. He reportedly recovered quickly upon receiving promise of a sum of money from the wealthy writer and popular philosopher Friedrich Heinrich Jacobi, to whom he had turned out of sheer desperation and without so much as the recommendation of acquaintance. As it turned out, he did not need to accept the gift, for at Herder's request the Duchess Luise von Sachsen-Weimar provided money for the return trip to Wandsbeck. In short order Claudius collected his family and few belongings, the *Görgeliana* and the four or five poems which he had managed to write during the year, and set out for home, where he arrived in early May.

The close of the episode in Darmstadt marked a turning point in Claudius's life. For over fifteen years he had observed from the side, then stood in the midst of cultural activity and for a short time in a center of sociopolitical affairs as well. In the process he had acquired a family and a name. The widespread attention given his departure from Darmstadt suggests a greater degree of publicity among contemporaries than one might imagine. Both as a writer and as a person he had served his apprenticeship, done journeywork, and even produced some masterpieces. His most recent venture and close brush with *Freund Hain,* however, had confirmed what he had known dimly since Jena and Copenhagen—he was not meant to live and to contribute to life in the world theater, for his existence drew its nourishment and sense ultimately from within himself and his home. These experiences impressed on him once again his feeling that the inadequacies of life in general lay not in a total failure to recognize truth but in an inherent inability in man to act on the recognition, which made itself most felt in the public arena.

Largely on the basis of these insights Claudius withdrew from direct involvement in public life to collect himself and to find his own way to benefit others. Together with Rebekka and their three daughters—Anna was born shortly after their return to Wandsbeck—he began a new phase in his life. Friends noticed an unfamiliar darkness of mood and forced quality of humor in him, which required considerable time to pass. The line "The earth is beautiful after all," which appears in "Nach der Krankheit 1777" [After my illness in 1777], represented at this point a hope as much as a conviction.[53] In response to Herder's apparent question regarding his future plans Claudius wrote, "Translations, publishing the continuation of Asmus, and—'Commit thy way!'"[54]

Later Travels and End of the Journey (1777–1815)

A look at the surface of Claudius's biography after 1777 would seem to justify, at least from this point on, its designation as a still life. Indeed, the generally uniform external course of his life renders a strictly chronological consideration unnecessary. Aside from occasional short stays in Bad Pyrmont for medical cures and two longer journeys Claudius spent the rest of his life in Wandsbeck. There can be no doubt that these years brought much joy and contentment in many respects into his home. Beneath the surface, however, the second half of his life was even more eventful than the first. During this time the Enlightenment entered its radical phase and reached its culmination. Immanuel Kant's critiques of pure and practical reason appeared, climaxing and initiating changes in philosophy and theology. Goethe and Schiller propounded a new art from Weimar and Jena. And, above all, the French Revolution broke out and spread all over Europe. All these events, as well as ones in his own home, represented continual threats to Claudius's physical and spiritual existence. He followed their development intensely and, moreover, responded to them in his own way—his writing.

As early as 1778, when Book III of the collected works appeared, Claudius made good his promise to Herder. Interspersed with numerous separate publications, Books IV through VIII followed at irregular intervals until 1812. Decreasing over the years, the returns from the works were not sufficient to cover the costs of supporting the growing family. During the late 1770s and early 1780s Claudius sought to augment this income by translating a number of works and tutoring Jacobi's sons. However, his situation remained precarious, for eight more children were born between 1779 and 1794.[55]

In view of these circumstances the step which Claudius took in 1781 appeared questionable indeed. To the amazement of his friends and the initial shock of Rebekka, he borrowed enough money to buy a large, vacant house just off the main road to Lübeck. Behind the house lay an area planted with lindens, a vegetable garden, and a fruit-tree orchard as well as a meadow for two newly acquired cows. Here, Claudius had room not only to play with his many children and to entertain friends but also to raise the essentials for the daily fare. While the move was daring, it proved to be necessary. For Claudius and his growing family country life had an entirely different meaning than for the shepherds and shepherdesses of Versailles and other European courts.

Claudius's faith in the future turned out to be not entirely unjustified. His friends continually helped him through hard times. Haugwitz made some gifts of money and during Claudius's visit to Silesia in 1784 introduced his friend to Count Gustav von Schlabrendorff, who granted him an annual sum for a few years. Claudius himself turned to Crown Prince Frederick of Denmark, who in 1785 made a similar gesture. His financial worries were eased considerably for a number of years when the Crown Prince named him First Inspector of the newly founded bank in Altona, near Hamburg, in 1788. More a sinecure than a regular position, the well-paid office required only that Claudius spend a few weeks each year helping check the bank's books. Some critics have viewed Claudius's dependence on the Danish court as the determining factor for his political stance during the tumultuous period which followed the French Revolution.[56] We shall see that this was not at all the case. In any event, Claudius for some time enjoyed a heretofore unknown financial security. It was certainly in part due to this that his good humor gradually returned to characterize much of his later life.

Yet, Claudius's spirit was tried over and again even during this time of relative prosperity—and not only by events in the world beyond Wandsbeck. His mother followed Pastor Claudius into death in 1780. In 1788 the second son bearing his given name died, and his beloved daughter Christiane passed away in 1796. Even the security of his income from Copenhagen disintegrated temporarily in the confusion of the war years, when the aging Claudius and Rebekka were forced to seek safety in emigration and the good services of relatives and friends.

In the meantime developments took place in Claudius's friendships. While never meeting personally, Claudius and Hamann continued a warm exchange of letters until the latter's death in 1788 and stood as godparents for each other's children. Hamann remained drawn to Claudius's character and unique brand of positive Christianity, which came to the fore increasingly in the successive volumes of *Asmus*. Jacobi continued to appreciate the kindred spirit he found in Claudius, despite or because of his own, more troubled religious life. However, it was precisely this religiosity which led to cooler relationships with Voß after 1778, and even with Herder. Each responded in his own way to the march of the Enlightenment, but both shared a distaste for the increasing fanaticism and mysticism which they saw in their old friend and his work.

During the 1780s and 1790s these friendships were augmented by newer ones, in part intensifications of older acquaintanceships. Through Jacobi, Claudius came into contact with a number of intensely religious Catholics living in and around Münster. After years of spiritual turmoil and a period of study with the Neo-Platonic Dutch philosopher Frans Hemsterhuis, Princess Amalia Galizyn finally settled near the Westphalian city. Here, she became the center of a theologically, intellectually, and socially active group with mystical leanings, which included the educational reformer Franz Egon von Fürstenberg, his colleague Bernhard Overberg, and the student of Eastern religions Johann Friedrich Kleuker. Still inwardly restless, she traveled to Wandsbeck expressly to meet Claudius, whom Jacobi had recommended as an exemplary Christian.

Claudius's long relationship with the Schimmelmann family and his growing friendship with Friedrich Leopold von Stolberg led him into even closer contact with the noble circle around Count Friedrich von Reventlow's estate Emkendorf in central Holstein. These and other noble families of the area, united by world-view as well as by marriage and friendship, formed the cultivated political and spiritual center of the region, with which the group in Münster also established friendly ties. Claudius and Rebekka were not the only members of bourgeois origin. Jacobi and later Schönborn, the philosopher and son-in-law of Wieland, Karl Leonhard Reinhold, as well as the publisher Friedrich Perthes, who eventually married Caroline, were among the highly educated products of the middle class who found refuge here. And refuge it was indeed. Emkendorf represented an asylum where differences of class and confession were less important than the common resistance to the spiritual, intellectual, and in time military invasion from both at home and abroad.

During these later years Claudius devoted more and more of his time to private study. He continued to keep abreast of the major works of German literature, especially those by his old friends Hamann, Herder, and Jacobi. Socrates, Plato, Bacon, Newton, and Robert Boyle also retained their attraction or grew even dearer. He limited his reviews to works by these contemporaries and translated shorter and longer pieces by the older writers. However, the new friends from Münster and Emkendorf were accompanied by new spiritual friends. Princess Galizyn sent Claudius works by St. Augustine and the Pietist poet Gerhart Tersteegen, while he in turn recommended Angelus Silesius and Johannes Tauler, among other mystics, to her. From the time of his return from Darmstadt to the last years of his life he spent many hours translating works by the Abbé Jean Terrasson, Andrew Michael Ramsay, Louis Claude de Saint Martin, Fénelon, and Pascal, all of which appealed to him because of their deeply religious character, colored to a greater or lesser extent by Pietism and Mysticism.[57] Urged onward by Hamann, Herder, and his new friend Kleuker, Claudius familiarized himself with the latest writings on Eastern religions.

The Claudius myth not only has Claudius leading an idyllic existence but, due in large part to his new friendships among the nobility and the religious of past and present, also becoming narrower in character and outlook. One is reminded here of Wieland's supposed "grand metamorphosis" during the 1760s, which has only recently been placed in a more adequate light.[58] Claudius's own alleged metamorphosis has long been disproven; Loofs demonstrated sixty-seven years ago that his position underwent no essential change.[59] The reasons for the longevity of the misinterpretation are complex and lie in part in the fact that Claudius's art, if not his poetics, did indeed change.

At least as early as Book IV and certainly by Book V one becomes aware of a more serious tone, of greater length in the prose pieces and something new in their style, and of correspondingly less space devoted to poetry. One notices an increased preoccupation with various aspects of religion and politics and poetics as well. Claudius had complained to Herder even in 1774 that his comic vein was running dry.[60] Since 1777 he had been free from the constraints of journalistic brevity and the need to appeal to the broadest possible audience and had been able to pursue more primary interests. These factors surely contributed to the changes noted. However, the less tangible but all-pervasive influences mentioned at the beginning of this section were likely more determining. A closer look at their consequences for Claudius's religion, with which his politics and poetics are inextricably entwined, will prove illustrative.

Herder once described Claudius's early work as being almost devoid of content but made for certain strings of the heart which are seldom stirred.[61] He was only partially right. The works which appeared in the newspapers and *Asmus I–II* certainly offer little fodder for doctrinal interpretation. Tacitly, however, they do reveal a primary and intuitive, rather than rational, experience of life which is specifically religious and Christian in character. And they express it often in a highly emotive, indirect language corresponding to the nature of the experience. Moreover, they presuppose similar experience in the reader for any adequate understanding. That is to say, they assume an experiential norm. In its absence, the language, if not the experience behind and in it, loses its justification as a means of communication.

And precisely here lies the crux of the problem. During the first half of the eighteenth century theologians of the predominant Wolffian school had used reason merely to demonstrate the truth of received religion. By the time Claudius began to write, however, the so-called Neologists were employing it to support "natural" religion. And in the 1780s and 1790s, with Kant's *Religion innerhalb der Grenzen der bloßen Vernunft* [Religion within the limits of reason alone], reason attained the status of a theological non plus ultra.[62] Claudius followed this development with the greatest attention. He later wrote in retrospect, "I could not believe that it was possible . . . to offer such things and represent them as wisdom to other people . . . still less that one could mock an existing religion in such a way to its face."[63] He gradually realized that all this was indeed possible. As the cognition of faith and revealed religion fell more and more into discredit, Claudius could no longer presuppose the experiential norm which had lain silent behind his earlier writing.

His recognition of a drastically new state of affairs, coupled with his sense of responsibility for the spiritual as well as material welfare of his fellow men, led Claudius to considerations similar to the following.[64] Examination of one's personal experience, it is evident, may or may not disclose an awareness of divine presence. Even if such introspection is fruitless, however, there are at least two "objective" ways of knowing the existence of divinity. One may consider man's current position in the world, and one may study the record of man's progress to this point, which abounds with testimonies to this awareness and its formative power on individuals and society.

These reflections were not lost on Claudius, for they brought about basic changes in his art.

To the last years of his life Claudius continued to cast his experience of transcendence as well as varied aspects of earthly existence in the affective language of lyric poetry, creating some of his best and most characteristic poems. Traces of his youthful ironic prose style are seen occasionally in both poetry and prose. In general, however, he found the vehicle of his early work inappropriate for the present enterprise. While retaining certain features of his old style, he turned more and more to the language of rational discourse.

In this mode of expression Claudius took extensive stock of contemporary life in numerous tracts, dialogues and correspondences, and even verse satires. His *Auch ein Beitrag über die neue Politik* [Another contribution on the new political system] of 1794 criticizes the French Declaration of Human Rights, while *Von und mit* [By and with, 1796] attacks the intrusion of rationalistic philosophy into the domain of theology.[65] Ultimately, his quarrel with Goethe and Schiller in the *Anti-Xenien* [Anti-Xenia] of 1797 must be seen in this light.[66] Claudius abhorred any glorification of form, whether philosophical, political, or literary, over the substance of life, for he felt it distracted man from his most essential, spiritual concerns. He thus sensed a presumptuous, fundamentally immoral force at work in the "empty aestheticism" of the Weimar Classicists. Whatever the immediate bone of contention, he attributed the malaise of the age, which culminated in twenty-five years of confusion and misery during the French Revolution and the Napoleonic Wars, to a significant breach with the spiritual traditions of the past. The old religious, political, and cultural institutions of Europe and their transcendental foundation, he felt, had for centuries provided stability for individuals and for society in Europe, and only a return to them—albeit in their true form—could restore the lost balance.

As a corollary of his inventory of present-day life Claudius stressed the continuing role of the Christian tradition in man's existence. In numerous letters to Andres and other pieces he gave detailed treatment to Christ, John the Baptist, and the stories of revelation and religious ceremonies as well as to issues such as conscience, faith, and salvation.[67] He left his children a moral legacy in *An meinen Sohn Johannes* [To my son Johannes, 1799] and composed a personal confession of faith for them in his *Einfältiger Hausvater-*

Bericht über die christliche Religion [A simple fatherly account of the Christian religion, 1803].[68]

All these works naturally entail an historical perspective. In others, Claudius searched even more widely into the past, in part beyond the Christian tradition, for traces of an awareness of divine presence like his own. The translations of Socrates, St. Martin, and others, mentioned earlier, are results of this quest. To these he added pieces from ancient Greece and Rome as well as passages from ancient Hindu and Chinese holy texts.[69] In these latter translations and his own extensive *Eine asiatische Vorlesung* [A lecture on Asia, 1803] he sought to establish the fundamental similarity and truth of all religions and the role of Christianity as the fulfillment of all previous spiritual experience.[70]

Exponents of the Enlightenment and Classicism gave Claudius and his late work a heated or indifferent reception due to the imagined and real changes and deficiencies in his character and writing. Often enough he wrote in self-defense or in support of others, for he and like-minded men came increasingly under attack by these individuals. Their recent friends have responded in a similar fashion. Claudius's production during this time was largely an attempt to fight fire with fire, to justify the life of the spirit by way of demonstration rather than to allow it to speak for itself. It was certainly in part an unequal struggle, and one may find the relatively infrequent poetry more compelling than the extensive prose. However one views the success of the attempt—and the opinions vary—it is important to remember that it was made expressly to affirm the primacy of individual spiritual experience, which was always Claudius's point of departure and return. His position on religion, politics, and aesthetics did not change. It was rather the times and with them the perspectives of perhaps the majority of leading thinkers which changed and seemed to demand more explicit formulations of long-held attitudes and views. Claudius did not *become* narrower, and he *was* narrow only to the extent to which one considers his Christian world view itself narrow. The criticism of detractors—and the praise of admirers as well—typically hinge on a personal response to this problem.

While the enlighteners turned their backs on Claudius, the Romantics offered him a warm welcome. By the early years of the new century they had already produced some of their most significant work and revealed an approach to life which, despite differences in detail and expression, was entirely compatible with his own. Claudius formed an intimate relationship with the painter and theoretician Philipp Otto Runge and wrote a moving poem on his early death; through him he became acquainted with the young artists Asmus Jakob Carstens and Johann Friedrich Overbeck.[71] The philosophers Franz Xaver von Baader, Henrik Steffens, and Friedrich Wilhelm Joseph von Schelling as well as the writers Ernst Moritz Arndt and Joseph von Eichendorff acknowledged their spiritual kinship to him. Friedrich Schlegel, a key figure in the German Romantic movement, himself approached Claudius for contributions to his *Deutsches Museum* [German museum]. And in her famous study of German culture *De l'Allemagne* Madame de Staël expressed respect for Claudius's earnest cheerfulness, which she found akin to English humor, and for the truth and sincerity of his sentiments.[72] The younger generation possessed a religious sensibility in general foreign to the older. Claudius saw in its representatives sympathetic spirits, while they in turn looked up to him as a prophet and defender of their values during an age of revolution, rationalism, and atheism.

Throughout his later years of family life and study Claudius maintained his widespread correspondence and frequently enjoyed visits from his younger and older friends. Indeed, his home became a place of pilgrimage for many, some of them the idly curious. He once received a traveling scholar in silence, led him to one of the cows behind his house, and with a symbolic flourish quietly swatted a number of flies from its hide with his cap.[73] On another occasion he met a lady before his door in his nightcap and assured her that Herr Claudius was not at home.[74]

While his humor never deserted him, Claudius became more withdrawn and at times irritable as events in the world beyond Wandsbeck took their course. He frequently waited impatiently at the door for the arrival of the daily newspaper. Caroline and her family as well as most of his other daughters remained close by in Hamburg or Wandsbeck. Anna, however, eventually followed her husband into territory occupied by the French. And his sons' studies, which later led three to the ministry and one to the mayoralty of Lübeck, for the time being carried them, too, far from the security of home.[75]

In the summer of 1813 the Wars of Liberation finally threatened even "idyllic" Wandsbeck, driving the seventy-three-year-old Claudius and his aging Rebekka from one place to the next for almost a year.[76] Due to the suspension of Claudius's salary they were compelled for the last time to live as best they could from the generosity of friends and relatives. Claudius's health began to suffer, as much from his divided political allegiance as from the rigors of the journey. Denmark and with it Holstein had been forced into an alliance with France, so that the liberation of his beloved Germany meant the defeat of his equally beloved Danish king. When the circumstances of the war allowed his return in May 1814, he was emotionally as well as physically exhausted.

Claudius's health deteriorated gradually over the following months, and as his condition worsened in December he moved into Caroline and Perthes's home in Hamburg to be closer to his physician. He spent his final weeks in meditation and prayer, waiting calmly and yet with anticipation for the end and "better times." At one point he said to his son-in-law, "I've thought about these hours my whole life long. Now they're here, but I still understand as little as in my healthiest days about how it will all end."[77] Claudius died on 21 January 1815 and was buried four days later in Wandsbeck.

Chapter Two

The Major Motifs

Religion: Self-Imposed Separation

In an introductory study such as the present one there is no room for an exhaustive treatment of any of Claudius's motifs, least of all religion.[1] A brief summary of the religious substance of many complete pieces, not to mention countless passages and allusions in other texts, would itself fill a volume. On the whole, Claudius's beliefs coincide with those of all Christianity and may thus be assumed to be familiar. However, his emphasis of certain of them lends his faith a quite personal character. Moreover, he applied their consequences in a remarkably consistent manner to all other areas of concern, which appear as the remaining motifs of his work. These facts suggest the need to point out here and in the following section at least two of the dominant features of his religion.

Claudius's deep sense of man's self-imposed separation from God was especially significant, both in primarily religious and more mundane matters. For Claudius, man's very real but imperfect communion with God, which has existed at all times, results in a certain relativity in any expression of divine awareness. The experience of God's existence, for example, engenders a need to live in accord with its content. It changes man inwardly, manifesting itself in a way of life and an attitude toward life.[2] That is, it leads to morality. The key words here are "way" and "attitude." The highly personal nature of religious experience creates a broad range of possible moral behavior, which due to its origin will nevertheless be essentially the same. The general way of life and the attitude toward it are thus more important than any codified rules of conduct. In the final analysis morality is for Claudius a derivative of religious experience, not an end in itself, which explains in part his rejection of Kant's categorical imperative.[3]

This relativity extends to all historical, institutionalized expressions of religious experience—to all the religions of the world, including Christianity, as well as to all their holy ceremonies and scriptures. The insight into this relativity gave Claudius a keen sense for the symbolic nature of all such manifestations and for the truth behind them all as well. He once described the world's religions as children of one father, differing in appearance but bearing familial traits, and was tireless in combating religious and confessional zealotry.[4] Time and again he stressed the importance of liturgy and revelation as sensual and thus comprehensible signs of the spiritual and ultimately incomprehensible.[5] Just as often and frequently in the same passages, however, he underscored his view that these are "news of the thing," not the thing itself.[6] The form is always arbitrary, but the essence made palpable by it is not.[7]

Claudius's attitude toward general expressions of religious experience determined his response to those of individuals of both past and present. In contrast to many of his contemporaries he was unwilling to exclude "heathens" from the possibility of salvation; in Socrates and other representatives of classical antiquity he indeed saw models of "Christian" conduct.[8] While retaining his affiliation with the Protestant church throughout his life, he was always able to praise Catholics and criticize members of his own confession.[9] His long life and activity in the world of letters brought him into contact with men of widely varying religious persuasions and occasionally of none at all. He met each individually and sought out his approach to life rather than any formal allegiance.[10]

Like his writing, Claudius's tolerance was a living reality. When Friedrich Leopold von Stolberg converted to Catholicism in 1800, his old, enlightened friends Jacobi and Voβ scorned his presence and vented their indignation and, one must add, sincere despair in the harshest words.[11] Even Klopstock would receive him only on the condition that the conversion not be mentioned. While not enthusiastic about the step, Claudius on the other hand maintained the old warm relationship with his friend for the rest of his life. Claudius's tolerance reached an end only where intolerance toward the religious experience and expression of others began.

While certainly influenced in varying degrees by the main religious currents of his time, Claudius was no orthodox, Rationalist, Pietist, or Mystic. One might best describe his religion as a very broadly conceived and personally accentuated version of Luther's own faith. Claudius parted ways with his precursor in his emphasis on the primacy of experience and rebirth. However, he shared with him belief in the fundamental separation between God and man and the role of Christ and grace in the process of reunion. The most appropriate label for his attitude is perhaps Dietrich Bonhoeffer's term "Christian worldliness."[12]

Reason and Philosophy: Pretenders to the Throne

Claudius's work abounds with direct and indirect statements on the place of reason and philosophy in life. When considered together, they disclose a basic concern for and attitude toward the possibility and nature of knowledge, or what may without undue exaggeration be called Claudius's epistemology. This concern and attitude grew organically out of his faith; indeed, many of the most important expressions are made in connection with religion.

Claudius's views on epistemology proceed from his belief in the presence of divinity in the human soul. He felt that man can gain direct knowledge of God's existence and being *only* through this link. Such knowledge is for him experiential in nature and manifests itself as feeling, emotion, or instinct, terms which he uses interchangeably.[13] Yet, the impressions of the soul are subject to the influence of multitudinous earthly stimuli, so that the knowledge thus obtained is imperfect.[14] Aside from the soul man possesses nevertheless no faculty for immediate perception of absolute truth. In this most essential regard knowledge derived from reason and philosophy is secondhand.[15]

The key to understanding Claudius's position, however, lies not in the proposition "either faith or reason," religion or philosophy, but rather in what he felt was the proper relationship between the two. As early as the *Adreß-Comptoir-Nachrichten* he says that head and heart should work together, illustrating their mutual dependence in the metaphor of the Houses of Lords and Commons.[16] Commons introduces all legislation, but Lords must give it the seal of approval. He later described their complementary nature in the image of a man and wife, who must remain together if legitimate children are to be born.[17] The offspring of this marriage are common-sense actions, a brood for which Claudius had the most paternal feelings. Thus, reason played a very important role in organizing and guiding knowledge obtained from the ultimate source.

However—a word encountered frequently in the present context—while head and heart *should* walk hand in hand, they usually do not. More often, the husband is a wife-beater, and in London Lords is at Commons's throat. In this abuse and usurpation Claudius saw both effrontery and danger. If the in part supernatural soul itself is numbed by the sensual world, how completely anesthetized must reason be, which is totally at the mercy of nature's quackery?[18] Moreover, such arrogance leads man away from his most primary concerns into false security. For the way to religion does not pass through metaphysics, and there is no necessary relationship between formal learning and a moral life or final healing.[19] Both religion and life were wholes for Claudius which cannot be separated from their source without losing much of their substance.[20]

Nature and Earthly Life: The Faces of Janus

Claudius possessed an unusual ability to bring life to a near standstill, to live close to the passing moment, and then to capture its joy in the language of immediate experience or of reflection. In "Täglich zu singen" [To be sung daily] he sings,

Ich danke Gott, und freue mich
  Wie's Kind zur Weihnachtsgabe,
Daß ich bin, bin! Und daß ich dich,
  Schön menschlich Antlitz! habe;[21]

(I thank God and am as glad
  As a child with a Christmas present,
That I am, am! And that I have you!
  Fair human countenance.)

The vibrancy of such lines derives in the main purely from the human creature's momentary transport with the rush of life. Yet, it stems in part from a sense of intimacy with a meaningful universe as well. The relationship of God and man through nature implicit in this piece permeates numerous others, chief among them the various *Bauernlieder* ("farmers' songs"). In "Das Bauernlied," for example, Claudius writes the lines,

We plow and we scatter
  The seed upon the land;

> But their growth and flourishing
> Lie not in our hand.
> All good gifts
> Come from above, from God,
> Down from the beautiful blue sky.[22]

However, Claudius's presentation of this cosmic triangle is not always as positive as these pieces would seem to indicate. "Frau Rebekka mit den Kindern, *an einem Maimorgen*" [Frau Rebecca with the children, on a May morning], which expresses in general the theme of the *Bauernlieder,* ends with the following reference to God and nature:

> He dwells himself unseen within,
> And is hard to discover.
> Be pious, and seek him with all your heart,
> To see whether you may find him.[23]

We shall see that even "Abendlied," supposedly a consummate expression of unity, is far from unproblematic. Indeed, many of Claudius's works reveal a pessimism toward nature and earthly existence, a literal God-forsakenness, as abject as any encountered in the seventeenth or twentieth centuries. In the early *Impetus philosophicus* (1775) he writes,

> but the heart . . . seeks to return to *Eden* and thirsts and longs for it. And a veil was bound about *Psyche's* eyes, and she was led out to play blindman's buff. She stands and listens beneath the veil, runs toward every sound, and spreads out her arms. I implore you, daughters of Jerusalem: if you find my friend, tell him that I am lying sick with love.[24]

Book IV of the collected works contains two other prose pieces of great significance in this regard. In *Der Besuch in St. Hiob zu* ** [The visit to St. Job in **] Claudius gives an unusually objective and dark account of an imaginary call paid to an establishment for the physically and mentally ill.[25] When asked how he could bear to see such misery every day, an attendant replies, "Would there be less of it if I did not see it? And can it be seen here alone?" This answer and the allusiveness of the name of the institution suggest the general character of the statement made by the work. Claudius more than once symbolized the world as a hospital, in which the afflicted are cared for until their recovery in death.[26] The work immediately following bears the title *Verflucht sei der Acker um deinetwillen etc.* [Cursed is the ground for thy sake etc.] and represents a commentary on Genesis 3:17–19.[27] Claudius described the anguish of life so vividly here that the philosopher of pessimism, Arthur Schopenhauer, later recommended the piece as an expression of the essentially pessimistic spirit of Christianity.[28]

Like so many readers, Schopenhauer "received" Claudius selectively, isolating those works which tended to support his own view of the world. However, he deserves credit for having seen in Claudius and Christianity what many others overlooked. Claudius's response to nature and earthly life was highly ambivalent and proceeded from a very real potential in Christianity, especially Protestantism. Despite the inner relationship between God and man and the possibility of communion between them, the distance separating them and the final uncertainty of grace could be overwhelming. For Claudius, the sense of union is not an ever-present state of being but rather a fleeting occurrence to be striven after constantly.

Claudius once wrote that the divine spirit is stamped in all matter and thus can be perceived in it.[29] Nature is a writing, and each creature, man the most important of them, is a letter. Each bears a trace of God and serves as his messenger to remind us of or tell us something about him. The senses themselves are seemingly unending sources of pleasure. As phenomena, however, nature and all creatures and their sensual experience carry their fundamental flaw within. They can provide no direct knowledge of God or overcome radical evil. Like all religions and religious scriptures and ceremonies, they are not the essence but only an ambiguous means to it. This attitude had a profound influence on Claudius's literary style.

Death

Aside from the awareness of divine presence and its promise the fact of physical death was Claudius's most central experience. Death cast a long shadow over his entire life; one might say that he lived each of his days with one eye upon it. The intimate relationship between life and death in his personal existence is mirrored in their proximity as motif within his literary production. His work reveals the same ambivalence toward death as toward life and nature, and for the same reasons.

In many pieces Claudius presents death positively as a transition to external life, which reflects back on earthly existence as an ephemeral but highly meaningful interlude. In 1772, while still a young man, he described his joy at attending funerals: "When I see wheat being sown, I begin to think already of the stubble and the harvest dance. . . . It is a moving, sacred, beautiful sight to look a corpse in the face. But it must have no finery. The quiet, pale form of death is its adornment, and the traces of decay its necklace and the first cockcrow to resurrection."[30] In other works, however, the promise of future bliss fades tonally in the moan of earthly misery. Even in the early *Parentation über Anselmo* [Eulogy for Anselmo, 1778] Claudius can write the lines, "Everything is vain and transient after all, worry, fear, hope, and finally death!—The time will come, Andres, when they wrap us too in linen and lay us in a coffin. Let us do, my friend, what we would wish to have done and place our trust in God!"[31]

In still other pieces on death the prospect of eternal life holds no comfort or does not exist at all. In "Das betrübte Mädchen" [The sorrowful maiden], which appeared still earlier in the *Tändeleien und Erzählungen,* the vision of her lover's being with God offers no consolation for the grief-stricken young girl, who feels that he cannot possibly be happy without her.[32] And during the period of his greatest public activity in 1772 Claudius addressed a poem on Bernstorff's death to Schönborn, which contains the following lines:

> They've buried him, too, with the others,
> And he'll come to us never again!
> He's lying now in the grave and moldering,
> And he'll come to us never again!
> And so they will all be buried,
> And molder in the grave to dust!
> . . . .
> Oh! S., if, oh! if they buried you, too,
> And I sought and couldn't find you! —
> I'll offer him sacrifice and implore,
> That death may long spare you.[33]

The pieces and tendencies discussed to this point represent extremes in Claudius's experience and work; they are constitutive elements but not the entire edifice. A look at additional writings reveals a fundamental attempt, not to reconcile his ambivalence toward death, but rather to accept it and to make it constructive. This endeavor is apparent early in Claudius's treatment of the figure of death.

The Grim Reaper first comes into full view in the dedication to Books I and II of the collected works, which was reproduced in part in Chapter 1. Claudius was well aware of other figures of death. In *Wie die Alten den Tod gebildet* [How the ancients represented death] Lessing had suggested that *Mors,* the beautiful Greek youth with the lowered torch, represented the serenity offered by Christianity better than the Grim Reaper.[34] Herder had agreed.[35] Claudius was attracted to the figure as well as to its counterpart, *Somnos* ("Sleep"), as the dedication indicates. However, he retained the medieval representation. Having accompanied him throughout his childhood and youth, it had acquired very personal significance for him. Moreover, it embodied a side of death which *Mors* did not, namely, the terrifying side. For Claudius the Christian, death entailed the fulfillment of a meaningful life and reunion with God. It also brought an end to the anguish accepted as an unavoidable companion along the way to the goal. For Claudius, the Protestant waiting for grace, however, death possessed an element of uncertainty, which tended to vitiate the sense and suffering of life within the universal scheme. And the very real worldly joys as well as the basic drive to live made their claims on Claudius, the human being.

Consequently, Claudius chose to live with death in all its dimensions. Only by coming to terms with its negative aspects could he devote himself to the positive. This was a lifelong process, and the balance was always precarious, now gravitating to one side, now to the other. In any case, his approach to death had a formative effect on his life. With his physical end and its questions ever in mind he developed a delicate sensibility for all the movements of the heart and for the real, if not ultimate, value of life. Their presence enabled him to mold his life optimally as a justification of having existed and gave him a sense of mission. He once wrote,

> Death is a peculiar man. He strips the pied clothing from the things of this world and opens the eye to tears and the heart to sobriety! One can of course be bewildered by him and do too much of a good thing, and that is usually the case when one has done too little up to that point. But he is a peculiar man and a good professor of morality! And it is of great

profit to do everything one does as if one were sitting before his lectern and eyes.[36]

Claudius's attitude toward death exerted a creative influence on his work as well. Not least of all, it led him to a symbol of death unique in literature, *Freund Hain.*

Recognition of the darker side of Claudius's view of life and death should not lead one to question his religious faith.[37] As we shall see, his literary style itself forbids such doubt. His works must be read as responses of a long, highly sensitive life to a wide range of experience, each of which reflects a moment in the mood of the poet and man. In the final analysis, the Claudius *mit seinem Widerspruch* ("with his contradiction") is at least as sympathetic as either the idylist or the secret skeptic.[38]

Love

In Chapter 1 we had the opportunity to observe the importance of marriage and family in Claudius's life. Few German poets have drawn on their rich sources so often or expressed their joys and sorrows so compellingly. These wells of experience were for him perhaps the least troubled of all. Like the rest, however, their origin and ultimate meaning lay in the realm of spirit.

Little is known of Claudius's youthful affairs of the heart. Whatever his real or imagined experiences may have been, his early work from the *Tändeleien und Erzählungen* to Books I and II of *Asmus* is replete with variations on the motif of "romantic" love. Most do not rise above the emotional threshold or the occasional charm of Anacreonticism. A few criticize humorously the extravagances of related feelings, as does "Fritze," which appeared immediately after the review of Goethe's *Werther:*

> Now I don't want to go on living,
> The light of day is vile to me;
> For she has given Franz some cookies,
> But none to me.[39]

Still others, such as the three letters to the moon, themselves luxuriate in high sentimentality.[40]

Yet, by the time of *Der Wandsbecker Bote* other tones can be heard. In 1772 Claudius comments on Genesis 1:27, "Er schuf sie ein

Männlein und Fräulein" ("Male and female created he them"): "What strengthens my assumption is the peculiarity and incomprehensibility of love. You stand there and tremble speechlessly, and your heart begins to pound and your cheeks to glow, and you don't know how or why. And right where philosophy founders and reason has to scratch its head, where you hear a rustling but don't know where it's coming from or going, right there I sense the hand of God."[41] And following the birth of his first daughter he wrote "Als er sein Weib und's Kind an ihrer Brust schlafend fand" [On finding his wife and his child sleeping at her breast]:

Das heiß ich rechte Augenweide,
's Herz weidet sich zugleich.
Der alles segnet, segn' euch beide!
Euch liebes Schlafgesindel, euch![42]

(Now I call that a feast for the eyes,
The heart shares in it, too!
May he who blesses all bless you both,
You sweet sleepyheads, you!)

Over the years Claudius wrote a number of pieces celebrating the life and love he shared with Rebekka. The vision of the son he did not yet have and weddings and births in the families of friends and relatives provided the impulse for several joyous occasional poems. The deaths of loved ones in his own family and more distant circles moved him to write some of his most beautiful and significant works. He treated marriage and family in various connections throughout his work. As in the commentary on the passage in Genesis, however, Claudius always returns directly or indirectly to the spiritual realm. In *Neue Erfindung* [New creation] he describes his attempt to attune his family to the eternal process of birth, death, and rebirth by celebrating with them a festival for each season of the year.[43] For in the love of man and woman and of parents and children he saw a reflection of divine love for all mankind. His *Einfältiger Hausvater-Bericht* contains the words, "we know well, when we feel charitable, benevolent stirrings and sentiments in our heart, that somewhere there must be a wellspring of love, an essential benevolence, a *loving father*. . . .[44] The nature and extent of this love are perhaps most apparent in the short poem "Die Liebe" [Love]:

Die Liebe hemmet nichts; sie kennt nicht Tür noch Riegel,
Und dringt durch alles sich;
Sie ist ohn Anbeginn, schlug ewig ihre Flügel,
Und schlägt sie ewiglich.[45]

(There's nothing hinders love; it knows no lock or key,
And passes through all things;
It is without beginning, ever beat its wings and
Shall beat them endlessly.)

In the *Antwort an Andres auf seinen letzten Brief* [Answer to Andres's last letter] Asmus expresses admiration for his friend's ability to lose sight of his worldly happiness while viewing the stars: "It gladdens my soul every time I hear of a man who keeps his head in spite of his passions and can forget bride and groom for something better."[46] Claudius stops, looks, and dwells on all manifestations of love. At the same time he sees them within the context of eternity, where their importance, like that of all temporal things, becomes relative. Nevertheless, earthly love is for him the closest approximation to divinity possible in life and is thus the least problematic of all areas of his experience.

Society and Politics: *ordo amoris*

The political Claudius, like the religious Claudius, has been claimed by proponents of various ideologies as one of their own. He has been called everything from a German patriot and slave of princes to a precursor of National Socialism and, more recently, of socialism.[47] As is so often the case, lines taken out of context can appear to support completely contradictory conclusions. However, such misunderstandings at least have the virtue of pointing out the important role of sociopolitical thought in Claudius's life and work, which all too often has been forgotten in the myth of the idylist. Claudius devoted many entire pieces to society and politics and touched on these subjects in many others. In them he dealt with numerous general and specific issues of his time. He had very definite views on these subjects, which can be clearly discerned and placed historically. Yet, as unequivocal as they are, they require interpretative care to avoid false generalizations such as those above, not least of all due to the literary form in which Claudius cast them. And like all other positions on topics of major importance to man, they proceed from his religious world view.

Claudius's outlook on the history of mankind is illuminating in this regard. The eighteenth century witnessed the beginnings of recognizably modern historical thinking, and Claudius's friendship with Herder brought him close to its source in Germany. In *Auch eine Philosophie der Geschichte zur Bildung der Menschheit* [Another philosophy of history concerning the development of mankind, 1774] Herder argued against the Enlightenment's equation of historical development with progress.[48] At the same time, however, he attempted to show that man had been in a process of perfection since the age of the patriarchs according to God's plan. Claudius reviewed the work the year it appeared.[49] While expressing general approval and acknowledging Herder's teleological view of history, he suggests significantly that one should perhaps seek God's plan synchronically rather than diachronically. For him, truth has always been the same in one guise or another, and God's plan for mankind lies outside human history. He backs away from the breach between sacred and secular history potential in Herder's philosophy and manifest in Voltaire's.

Claudius's notion of the essential immutability of human history is complemented by his view of the basic unchangeability of human nature. This idea is implicit in his indirect comparison of Rome before the fall and the present age in "Ein Versuch in Versen" [An essay in verse] in 1773.[50] It is explicit in the preface to the third volume of his translation of Fénelon's religious works (1811), where he states, "Since human nature is always the same, however, and its possibilities, needs, and flaws are always identical or at least similar, aside from some regional and individual circumstances, man's consolation and counsel must naturally always be identical or similar as well."[51]

Traces of historical consciousness appear occasionally in the work. There is something of Rousseau in the suggestion that the ancients possessed more courage and energy than modern men.[52] On the whole, however, Claudius's understanding of man's walk through the ages is ahistorical. Indeed, he employs history to deny historicity.[53] For him, secular history is merely an extension of sacred history and its story of salvation.

This is apparent as early as 1778 in the sketch of the origin and nature of social and political life contained in *Nachricht von meiner Audienz beim Kaiser von Japan* [Report on my audience with the emperor of Japan], both thematically and formally one of Claudius's major works.[54] Here, Asmus says that God made all men brothers and that all are equal in death and in his eyes. He placed them on earth temporarily to live accordingly. Because of their natural weakness, however, they were unable to do so. Consequently, he chose the best and noblest among them to represent him as fathers to all other men. These are the emperors, kings, and princes. The subject owes his ruler the unconditional and unquestioning obedience due a father. The ruler, by the same token, is entrusted with the well-being of his subject both in this world and the next.

The social and political relationship outlined here reveals the interpenetration of sacred and secular history in Claudius's world-view and is as clear an expression of divine-right patriarchalism as one is likely to find. It also represents Claudius's understanding of the foundation and structure of the *ancien régime* in Europe. Claudius was acutely aware of the faulty construction of this edifice, as both this and other works indicate—a fact both under- and overestimated in critical commentary. The secular order presented in the work is an ideal rather than a literal description of reality. It is this ideal which underlies all his statements on society and politics. He harbored it years before accepting the sinecure from the Danish court and before the ideas of progress and perfectibility reached their first culmination in 1789. His rejection of the French Revolution and its ideals reflects no shift of position but rather a response to a menace to principles long cherished and asserted. The prospect of changing the sociopolitical form through which God's plan had apparently functioned over the centuries seemed ominous to Claudius indeed.

Auch ein Beitrag über die neue Politik is Claudius's most direct discussion of the events in France and one of his most systematic and important statements on politics and life in general. Here, as elsewhere, one may fault his premises; his faculty for historical thought and political detail was limited. However, he often made much of very little. He finds the individual articles of the Declaration of Human Rights generally true but in their generality too vague and open to later interpretation and abuse to serve as positive laws. They say everything and nothing and take with one hand what they give with the other. He is most convincing when reflecting on human nature in connection with politics. He says at one point that political institutions alone can make man neither happy nor good. Human evils cannot be eradicated simply by eliminating the forms in which they have traditionally appeared. He believes that man is too weak to govern himself, for there remains an unbridgeable gulf between even the best will and the corresponding action, both in the state and the individual. For Claudius, true freedom is spiritual rather than political in the first place. One can work toward this kind of liberty under any system and with no understanding of politics at all. If the individual begins the process of reform within himself, the reform of the state will evolve as a matter of course.

In the *Gespräche, die Freiheit betreffend* [Conversations on freedom], published even earlier in Book V and another major work on politics, Claudius centers his concept of freedom more directly within its spiritual context.[55] Even in the most reasonable form of government there are obstacles to pragmatic political freedom. They stem from the finitude of man and earthly life on the whole. Essential freedom, "the real England," lies in release from the flesh and union with God.

Precisely because he took his spiritually founded sociopolitical ideal so seriously, Claudius was far from advocating the *ancien régime* as it actually existed and had existed in most places. He understood himself as a friend and defender of the weak and abused, and his work abounds with criticism of the misuse of power. This criticism assumes various forms. He aims humorous but pointed barbs at the injustices of the strong in a number of fables and verse narratives. And in the newspaper he edited in Darmstadt the simple, loyal subject Görgel reminds his ruler of his duty indirectly by addressing him as if he already governed as he should.[56]

Claudius's sympathy for the downtrodden could lead him to strong attacks on political oppression. In the report on his visit to Japan, Asmus's discovery of a human skull and the vision of its living owner's torment elicit helpless rage.[57] However, it was the outbreak of the War of the Bavarian Succession in 1778 that inspired his most moving indictment. In a poem bearing the ironic title "Kriegslied" [Song of war], he included the verses,

> There's war! There's war! Oh angel of God impede it,
> And intercede for us!

Alas, there's war—and I desire
  That I not be to blame.
What should I do, if in my sleep with sorrow
  And bloody, wan, and pale,
The spirits of the slain came to me,
  And wept before me, what?
. . . .
    What value crown and land and gold and honor!
  They could not gladden me!
Alas, there's war—and I desire
  That I not be to blame.[58]

While the misuse of power provoked language such as this, benevolent rule prompted words of praise. When Frederick the Great and Maria Theresa ended the war over the Bavarian throne in 1779, Claudius published a poem in which he attributed their action, idealistically or in subtle suggestion, to concern for their subjects and reflection on their true duties.[59] And when the Austrian empress died the following year, he celebrated her as a peacemaker.[60]

Claudius's criticism and praise of the powerful, which have elicited such contradictory reactions, stem neither from a belief in mankind's maturity nor from an acceptance of carte-blanche authority. He was neither a revolutionary nor a lip server. They sprang basically from a deep, personal love for all mankind, a true humanism, which was at the same time a reflection of divine love. For Claudius, the family of man extended from the spiritual realm on down to the individual home and included both the single state and the different nations of the world. Nowhere in his work is there a sign of the nationalism of the nineteenth- or twentieth-century kind. What has been interpreted as such—his Bardic songs, for example—are expressions of patriotism in the sense of a love for familiar, German variations of universal human values. Claudius soon enough turned against even the Bardic movement, itself more culturally than politically nationalistic. He advocated war only in self-defense. His approach to the relationship of nations was fundamentally cosmopolitan, his criticism of France and England directed in part against precisely their breach of cosmopolitanism.[61] His divinely sanctioned sociopolitical ideal derived essentially from his concern for the material and spiritual welfare of all men.

From the distance of nearly two hundred years it is easy enough to say that Claudius should have been more farsighted and recognized the need for fundamental social and political change, especially given his Christian Humanism and keen awareness of current and past abuses of the *ancien régime.* It is not difficult to point out that he, unlike myriads of others, had the good fortune to live under relatively benevolent rulers. When immersed in the torrent of the time itself, however, an individual's vision is not infrequently less than clear. Many other Germans and Europeans repudiated the revolution in France, although at times for reasons different from those of Claudius. After welcoming its outbreak enthusiastically, Klopstock, Goethe, and most leading artists and intellectuals shuddered at its progress. Along with Wieland, Claudius was one of the few who immediately recognized its possible consequences. Given its course of development and the events of the war years, his conviction that man had not yet reached majority and his affirmation of a system which reflected this belief are entirely understandable. One may well be inclined to respect his sense for the fragility of all social and political life. Claudius's disregard for the influence of political form on human life is at least counterbalanced by his championing of living content.

Poetics: Trimming, Child's Play, and a Cup of Cold Water

Claudius never wrote anything remotely resembling a systematic exposition of artistic principle. His gifts and interests were primarily of a creative rather than an analytical nature. However, he was not at all without critical reflection. His numerous reviews of contemporary works in the newspapers and in the first books of *Asmus* reveal a fine and certain instinct for literary values. These and other works contain statements on and allusions to art, language, genius, and the artist, which allow one to deduce a coherent aesthetic attitude.

The term "sensibility," understood as "a reliance upon the feelings as guides to truth and conduct as opposed to reason and law as regulations both in human and metaphysical relations," goes a long way toward expressing a basic premise of the literary and intellectual avant-garde of the time with respect to both literature and life.[62] If we bring Claudius's epistemology to bear on it, the concept also goes a long way toward explaining his position in the discussion on poetics.

Man has access to ultimate truth for Claudius, we recall, through that remnant of divine nature resting in his soul since the fall. The knowledge thus acquired manifests itself experientially as intuition or emotion. When this experience finds appropriate linguistic expression, it assumes the form of metaphors, symbols, and all the other figures of poetry and prose which flow from and address primarily the senses and feelings.

Claudius himself employs such language in a very revealing piece entitled *Über das Genie* [On genius], which first appeared in *Der Wandsbecker Bote* in 1771.[63] Here, he writes, "In idle hours I often picture a language as a bundle of sticks, to each of which a spellbound princess or an unhappy prince has been affixed by magic."[64] Claudius's usage of imagery drawn from the fairy tale suggests his awareness and affirmation of the figurative and emotive dimension of language. It soon becomes clear that he finds the cognitive referents of words—the sticks themselves and their naming function—less attractive. Further along the reason for his preference is apparent: "It is said that in real sorcery, if one understands the craft, a princess can be released from her spell and a goblin or elf enchanted onto the stick in her place. It is certainly the same with languages. . . ."[65] From this imagery emerges Claudius's view of the power of figurative language to express truth and beauty, which are identical, and to distinguish them from their opposites.

The emotional nature of truth charmed by such language and its ultimately divine source are revealed in Claudius's enthusiastic review of Klopstock's *Oden* [Odes], both of which appeared in 1771.[66] After reproducing stanzas from his friend's "Der Erbarmer" [Father of mercy], in which Klopstock praises God ecstatically for saving mankind, Asmus asks, "Now is that foaming, *Vetter?* How do you feel after reading it? How do I feel? A *hallelujah* stirs in me, too . . . I'd like to tear the stars from the sky and strew them at the feet of the Father of Mercy and sink into the earth. That's how I feel!"[67] His cousin is somewhat less enraptured earlier in the review, where Asmus reports his idea that poems "must be clear, like a drop of dew, and heartfelt, like a sigh of love, especially since the whole value of contemporary poetry rests in this dew-drop clarity and the warm breath of emotion."[68] In a brief history of music which came out the same year Claudius objectively presents his belief in the original unity of divine inspiration, poetry, and music.[69]

He was firmly convinced of the truth and moral power of all art forms.

However, poetic language need not be hieroglyphic to be true. Claudius felt that the simple phrases and figures, rhythms, and motifs of the folk song, as it had been transmitted over the centuries, had borne and were still capable of bearing nature or truth. He cultivated them on a high level throughout his life; indeed, the folk song and related Protestant hymn were his major poetic forms. He also had great respect for everyday, colloquial speech and its reproduction in literature. In the humorous dedication of *Wandsbeck, eine Art von Romanze* [Wandsbeck: a kind of romance] to the Emperor of Japan he makes the serious statement, "Should His Majesty hear . . . the comment that my verses are strewn rather carelessly, I graciously request He bear in mind that they are intended to be strewn carelessly."[70] He himself spoke Low German at home and with friends. While only one complete work is written in dialect, he sprinkled expressions from his native tongue and various colloquialisms from the adopted High German throughout his work.[71]

For Claudius, as for his contemporaries, nature was a very broad concept. It could encompass at different levels all aspects of both the phenomenal and spiritual realms. The soul and emotion provided the connection between the two, as we have seen. Their linguistic expression, even in the most commonplace form, could thus be at once "natural" and true on both higher and lower planes. Consequently, Claudius very consciously cultivated colloquial language in his writings. This fact is important for a proper understanding of his stylistic change and his later prose works.

Claudius frequently expressed admiration for men who possessed the ability to fashion a language which could move their reader or spectator emotionally to recognition of truth. In *Über das Genie* he describes the man who recognizes the emotive power of language as a "Sunday's child, who can see spirits, while the other sees the stick and nothing more."[72] And when the Emperor of Japan asks what poets are, Asmus replies, "Bright, pure pebbles, which the beautiful sky and the beautiful earth and holy religion strike together so that sparks fly."[73]

Given Claudius's attitude toward language, art, and the artist discussed so far, it is not surprising that he rejected the normative-systematic poetics of Neo-Classicism. In a piece entitled *Steht Homer z. Ex. unterm Spruch des Aristoteles & Compagnie?* [Does Homer, e.g., stand under the judgment of Aristotle & company?] he answers his own question by referring to Christian Felix Weiße's *Romeo und Julia:*

> The question seems to me as comical as if it had occurred to someone, when the thrill and clamor of love and despair had grown quiet and the unfortunate enthusiast had died, to knock on the door of the tomb and to ask . . . whether Miss Juliet had played her role with expression and according to the rules of art. . . . A bunch of art critics and a year's worth of journalists piping wisdom must be dirt under the feet of the man who has a warm heart, wants earnestly to be useful, and has what it takes.[74]

Along with Klopstock's circle and the *Sturm und Drang* writers Claudius defended the concept of artistic freedom insofar as this meant the artist's right to depart from canons of rules for poetic creation. Such catalogs represented for him an impermissible rationalization of a basically emotional process. The individuality of emotional experience brings with it an individuality of expression, which should not be constrained by any preconceived, immutable laws. Rather than depending on such codified rules, the poet should rely on nature in the fullest sense of the word; for nature is the proper source and object of art. If the artist is true to his own response to nature, his expression will emerge of itself. Claudius's criticism of literature followed from these principles and is itself highly intuitive and individualistic.

At this point we must pause for a moment to note that the picture of Claudius's poetics drawn so far is only half complete. He indeed believed that art and the artist possessed significant potential and found this potential realized in works of all ages. At the same time he felt that both were subject to severe inherent limitations. These must be sketched if his views on the subject are to be fully understood.

We recall Claudius's belief that human emotions can be addressed not only by the soul but by all earthly phenomena. This interference impairs their capacity to communicate the originally clear impulses from the spiritual realm and thus makes them imperfect like all other things of this world. It follows that linguistic expression of emotional experience, itself an entirely temporal appearance, must be flawed as well. This idea permeated Claudius's attitude toward poetics from early on.

Claudius made an important general statement in this connection in the *Morgengespräch zwischen A. und dem Kandidaten Bertram* [Morning conversation between A. and the student Bertram] in Book VIII of the collected works: "For words are words, and one cannot be on one's guard enough against them. When they have *real* objects, everything goes fairly well and safely. But when they deal with abstract concepts the matter becomes thorny."[75] He then draws on a pertinent, systematic discussion by Bacon to support his contention and concludes, "And here words and phrases are the little Cartesian devils incarnate."[76] Language is relatively reliable where it reflects the objective and the close at hand. When it seeks to go beyond, however, whether in theology and philosophy as here or in literature, its inadequacy (indeed, its harmfulness) is everywhere apparent.

Claudius was highly skeptical of literary language, once referring to it as an "infamous funnel in which wine becomes water."[77] Even in the eulogy for Josias in 1760 he spurns the flourishes of the orator, saying that a sigh or tear speaks more eloquently; the first line of one of the poems written on this occasion reads, "Today I wish not to appear in poetic garb."[78] Such complaints about the impotence of poetic language were common in an age of sensibility. With Claudius and others as well, however, they were a matter of principle. In a letter to Andres in Book V Asmus says, "You write that he [John the Baptist] seems so great to you and yet you can't quite say why. That's really good, Andres. One often knows most just when one can't quite say why."[79] Language may proceed from ideas or emotions—from realities—but it is never identical with them. The objectivity of language itself precludes such identity, and there always remains an essential difference between them.[80]

Moreover, many poets seem to be unaware of this difference, equating their poetic productions with truth. Claudius may well have clapped his hands with glee on reading and later translating Socrates' words on poets. After going among them in his search for wisdom and knowledge, the sage says to his fellow Athenians, "But I am ashamed to tell you . . . that they wrote . . . not from the inspiration of wisdom but rather from a natural inspiration in a kind of enthusiasm like the prophets and soothsayers. For these, too, say many beautiful things but understand nothing of what they say. . . . At the same time I noticed, too, that because of their rhyming they believed themselves to be wise men in other things as well, but they were not."[81]

Not only do they fail to recognize the yawning gap between experience and language; poets frequently take it upon themselves to write in the absence of any experience at all. In *Ernst und Kurzweil, von meinem Vetter an mich* [Earnestness and pastime, from my cousin to me] in Book IV, for example, Asmus's cousin offers some comic exempla to show the difference between emotional earnestness and pastime. In one he writes,

> The sea is stormy . . . and the ship to the left [of a sketch included in the piece] . . . is about to sink. You are on the other ship and see your poor neighbors stretching out their hands and crying for help. Now, if you're an aesthetic soap boiler, then sit down and write an elegy on the sinking of the other ship together with how the people screamed and the kind of sympathy you felt, etc. But if your sympathy is earnest, then go to the skipper and ask him to risk the lifeboat. Hang the poet to the mast, so that he won't get in the way when you lower the boat, and climb in quickly and joyously with the other sailors to retrieve the poor people.[82]

Worst of all, many poets, even the best of them, lose all sight of the content of art and create a cult of form. In his review of Wieland's *Der neue Amadis* in 1771 Claudius cannot but acknowledge his bedazzlement at the author's stylistic virtuosity.[83] However, he absolutely rejects what he perceives as the immorality and even mockery of virtue in the work. Such considerations underlie his position in the heated controversy over Goethe's *Werther* during the early 1770s and his condemnation of Goethe and Schiller, the "aesthetic bagpipes," and their ideas during the late 1790s.[84] For Claudius, the content of literature, as of religion, politics, and all other areas of life, is far more important than form. And there is subject matter both proper and improper for literary treatment. Artistic freedom does not entail the liberty to be immoral. For this reason Claudius can criticize formally free works, such as Klinger's *Das leidende Weib,* and praise more conventional pieces, such as Lessing's *Emilia Galotti.*[85]

In view of the fundamental inadequacy and widespread abuse of the written word Claudius frequently recommends the self-sufficiency and purposefulness of silence. He fairly demolishes a contemporary, formal laudation of Christ: "Herr Bastholm asks right at the beginning, 'May I speak, when the seraphim are silent?' What good is the question? Why did he not remain silent instead? The silence of the seraphim is the true laudation of the Messiah, it or none at all. Anything else is sickening water soup. . . ."[86] To say many things is to profane them. Truth and language are of two entirely different orders of being, and silence is often the ultimate sign of reverence and wisdom. We shall see that Claudius was in this regard truly reverent and wise, for much of his work is an expression of meaningful silence.

Claudius's basic pessimism toward language is as pervasive as that of Maurice Maeterlinck or Hugo von Hofmannsthal in more recent times. In view of this skepticism one may well wonder why he wrote at all. When asking this question, one should of course remember that neither Maeterlinck nor Hofmannsthal ceased to write because of their insight into the insufficiency of language. Yet, the latter did in fact give up one form of expression for another. And Claudius, too, altered his style in his later work. However, this shift resulted not from any change in his poetics, but rather from what he saw as a threat to it. A closer consideration of his view of the purpose of art will demonstrate this fact.

Our reading of Claudius indicates that the core of his poetics can be understood entirely in terms of the Horatian dictum "Et prodesse volunt et delectare poetae" ("Poets want both to instruct and to delight"). To be sure, he interpreted Horace in a different sense from many of his contemporaries. Rationalists saw the instructive function of literature as lying in part in the transmission of rationally conceived truths. The pleasure of literary art derived from the intellectual comparison of the artist's imitation of truth with truth itself. Literature and truth were thus two distinct entities, and literary form served the didactic purpose of conveying truth as well as activating the intellect of the reader as the faculty for perceiving it.

Claudius, on the other hand, found both the instructional and entertainment value of literature in its cultivation of sensibility. For he felt that the emotions are at once the bearers of truth and the source of pleasure. Literature fulfilled its raison d'être by evoking the truth and enjoyment of feeling and by exercising man's capacity to experience them. No less than the Rationalists, however, he saw an essential difference between literature and truth. For him, unlike the Classicists and Romantics, there is no truth inherent in artistically formed language. Words are entirely neutral and can be used for both the good and the bad. Moreover, the emotions themselves are not infallible and can be led astray as well as along the right path.

Consequently, everything depends on the thematic content of literature. Claudius's criticism of Wieland and Goethe and Schiller, indeed, his statements on form and content in all contexts, indicate that he was far more interested in what literature *does* than in what it *is*. His works disclose a keen sense for the interplay of form and content. However, literary form is legitimate for him only to the extent that it supports by enlivening literary content or truth. Claudius's approach to literature is thus as didactic, if in a different way, as that of Gottsched or, for that matter, of Goethe and Schiller. Like the former and contrary to the latter, in any case, he "commits" what New Criticism condemns as the "affective fallacy" and what some recent critics praise as engagement.[87]

While Claudius's attitude toward literary form and content is manifest in his early work, it is especially visible in his later writings. In the preface to Book VIII Asmus writes, "Readers will have to be content with word and expression. One can't help no longer being young when one is old. But as regards the content, which is after all the main thing in a writing, I think I've kept my word."[88] And in the *Valet an meine Leser* [Farewell to my readers] in Book VII Claudius alludes both to the dedication in Books I and II and Matthew 10:42: "Most of it is *trimming and child's play,* wound like a garland round my *'Cup of Cold Water,'* so that it might strike the eye more pleasantly."[89]

Claudius wrote for the sake of the cup of cold water, which he felt was increasingly being contaminated by the spirit of the time. Completely aware of his own limitations and those of his enterprise he understood himself more and more as a messenger and defender of religious truth.

Not only the cup of cold water, but the trimming and child's play as well were being defiled by the times. Consequently, Claudius turned increasingly from the predominantly figurative language and the frequently fragmented, impetuous syntax of his youth, which had proven particularly subject to abuse. In his later work he made a concerted effort to unite the language of emotion with the more measured idiom of natural, everyday language. Each was capable of bearing truth when used alone. How much more effective might they be if employed together?

Chapter Three

The Prose: Fragments of a Great Conversation

Claudius is known and represented in literary histories and anthologies chiefly as a poet. And it is true, as has recently been stated, that he is at his best in the lyric.[1] However, his achievement in prose is not at all negligible, as critical discussion seems to suggest. In a recent study of the satire of the period, for example, Claudius's name is not so much as mentioned in passing.[2] Yet he employed some of the standard forms of the time in his own original way, frequently reaching and occasionally rising above the level of accepted satirists of the period. And his success in prose is not limited to the satire alone.

The allusion to Goethe's famous description of his life work in the title of the chapter is not entirely fortuitous.[3] First of all, Claudius's prose is indeed fragmentary, not least of all in the sense that many of the individual pieces, written in an age not known for shortness of breath, are relatively brief. More importantly, as we have seen, his work was a self-conscious apology for his life. The letters and dialogues of his alter egos can in some instances be read as meditation or soliloquy. However, these two of his major prose vehicles are conversational forms par excellence, which explains the departure in our title from Goethe's designation of his work. In a broad sense the other important prose forms and the poetry as well represent in part Claudius's attempt to share himself, to confess his feelings and ideas on both ephemeral and universal issues to his reader.

A Man of Many Masks: The Fictional Circle

Over the years Claudius developed his own distinctive manner of self-communication. With an ever-increasing certainty of hand, he expressed his experience of life through and within a circle of fictional characters which served as a framework for most of his production, both prose and poetry, and for its constituent parts. Because of its formal and thematic significance we shall consider its nature and functions in detail before proceeding to the body of the prose.

Earlier we mentioned the influence of the moral weeklies of Addison and Steele on European literature during the eighteenth century. They and the most successful of their imitations are distinguished from other periodicals most notably by the presence of a fictitious group of correspondents or interlocutors.[4] This circle is comprised of individuals with different, clearly delineated personalities, who discuss various matters from their own peculiar point of view. The reader is implicit as the peruser of the pages or fictionalized as the recipient(s) of the letters.

Claudius reveals his debt to the genre in his creation of similar fictional circles in the *Adreß-Comptoir-Nachrichten, Der Wandsbecker Bote,* and finally in the collected works. By the time of the appearance of the first two volumes of *Asmus* he had worked out problems of inconsistency in his characters and point of view and had begun to realize the potential of the fictional framework. He was able to sustain a uniformly personal, conversational relationship with his reader, whether his subject and approach to it were serious or humorous. This relationship and his modulation of it are a precondition for much of the entertainment and edification specific to Claudius's art. More importantly, however, he was able to create distance between himself and his reader on the one hand and the content of his works on the other. This fictional realm provided Claudius with the means of treating in his own way a stylistic phenomenon central to his own work and the art of the time.

Perspectivism had long played a prominent role in both thought and the arts and fairly flourished in the literature of the eighteenth century, especially in the work of Wieland.[5] Claudius's production, too, bears testimony in different ways to his sense of the value of perspectivism. His usage of it reveals an important aspect of his contact with the age—its influence on him and his repayment of the debt.

As we have seen, it is characteristic particularly of Claudius's early work that content is not presented objectively, but rather subjectively by fictional writers or speakers and readers or listeners, both present and implied, who possess different personalities. Despite similarities Asmus and *Vetter* differ from each other; often, they are at odds on a given subject. While sharing certain traits with them, Andres, too, is his own man. If any doubt as to his function as "the reader" is left after *Der Wandsbecker Bote,* it is dispelled by one of the letters to him written specifically for *Asmus I–II,* where the messenger writes, "I can't just shoot out into the wild blue yonder. I have to have someone to aim at, and you're so comfortable and easygoing, not too dumb and not too smart, and you're not ill-natured."[6] Rector Ahrens, Görgel, and a host of minor or major figures who appear only once or twice all present their often widely differing views, openly or implicitly, on various matters.

Consequently, one cannot say unequivocally that this or that character is Claudius or that this or that statement represents his view. In the dedication to Books I and II Asmus and his cousin are described as being identical; *Vetter* is even given the name "Matthias Claudius."[7] This occurs, however, within an already fictional realm where little can be taken at face value. *Vetter* is the author in the same sense that Asmus, Görgel, and a number of far less respectable characters are—Matthias Claudius and his inner world broken through a multi-faceted prism. Neither can one say that Andres is identical to the vast number of different empirical readers. He is fictional—the reader as Claudius would like to have him and toward whom he directs his writing in order to form his real readership.

Claudius was an intensely private man despite his humor and love of camaraderie. His inner life and that of others were sacred to him and not for public consumption. Due in part to this attitude he became a man of many masks, for they provided a degree of anonymity unattainable in other authorial postures of the time. Moreover, they offered a measure of personal distance between deepest emotion and statement.

There is another, perhaps more important reason for Claudius's perspectivism. We recall from the preceding chapter that the subjective, intuitive nature of the perception of truth or knowledge implies a fragmentation of its empirical existence. No individual, no system, no age is capable of comprehending it in its entirety. Yet, various individuals do catch glimpses of it here and there; and when these are viewed together, one sees a more detailed, if scarcely complete, picture of the whole. The greater apprehension of truth through approaching it from numerous points of view is to a great extent the stylistic sense of Claudius's fictional circle and perspectivistic usage of it. The total statement of a given work and the real Claudius typically emerge from a comparison and weighing of the various perspectives presented. Not infrequently, the meaning of a piece can be completely understood only with reference to the fictitious framework in which it appears. In the broad sense mentioned at the beginning of the chapter, even works not structured by perspectivism—certain reviews, prefaces, translations, and even the poetry—are parts of an overall endeavor to illuminate life from as many standpoints as possible. In this regard the designation of Claudius's work as fragments of a great conversation assumes another, vital dimension.

At this juncture it may be well to reflect for a moment on the fact that perspectivism, both as an approach to life or truth and as a literary technique, is quite rationalistic, based largely on additive, comparative, and contrastive—in general, analytical—thinking. Much of Claudius's early work exhibits highly emotive language and free structures and may rightly be called poetic prose. Even in his earliest work and then throughout his life, however, many pieces disclose blatantly rational language and formal principles. Often, the two modes of expression appear together.

There is an apparent inconsistency in the fact that Claudius very frequently criticizes the rationalistic approach to life and art through rationalistic means. However, the inconsistency is only apparent. For Claudius, we remember, felt that reason was essential in assimilating and directing knowledge gained through the primary source. Those who speak disparagingly of the irrationalistic Claudius should perhaps consider his very real and acknowledged debt to his time. He entertained and enlightened his reader through both emotion and intellect.

The equally real change in Claudius's later style is signaled by changes in the fictional circle in the collected works. From Book V on the frequency of appearance by his personae decreases sharply. Moreover, he largely abandoned the indirectness of his earlier satire and poetic prose. When the times threatened his inner sanctum and that of others, Claudius was willing to dispense with his masks and to reveal himself more directly to his readers—and the critics. He approached his medium in a more openly and consistently rationalistic fashion, albeit still in support of an entirely different order of experience. Although other themes and forms of expression figure here as well, *Asmus* thus became a highly religious, formally rationalistic, and, to that extent, a narrower organ.

However, Claudius published a number of works individually or in other organs and never included them in *Asmus,* as he was wont to do with such pieces.[8] The politics and philosophy discussed in these works along with religion create a somewhat broader thematic scope than that of the collected works. Furthermore, new fictional characters in the manner of the earlier epistolary and dialogue forms compensate to a degree for the attrition in *Asmus* by providing greater formal range.[9] The impression made by the Winkler edition, which contains these additional pieces, is different from that of the collected works alone, as they originally appeared.

The multiplicity of Claudius's prose presents problems of selection and arrangement in an introductory study. His aphorisms, prefaces, translations, and letters are numerous, varied in theme and style, and in their own right significant. In later life he wrote a number of pieces closely resembling the Protestant sermon.[10] Over his long career he cultivated the literary epistle, dialogue, dramatic narrative, and treatise; during the relatively short period of his journalistic activity alone he wrote some one hundred reviews and feuilletons. Even these major genres create difficulties, however, due to an extensive overlapping of forms, motifs, and devices among them. The breakdown of the barriers between the old literary kinds during the eighteenth century is by now a familiar phenomenon.[11] Claudius's prose defies any comprehensive systematization, his typical forms representing his own *genres mêlés,* and it would be contrary to their spirit to attempt to classify them too rigidly. What follows, accordingly, are individual samples of some of Claudius's chief prose forms, grouped loosely around various stylistic treatments of motifs.[12] While themes such as earthly life, death, and love are by no means neglected in the prose, they find more frequent expression in the poetry and for that reason are treated in the following chapter.

A Philosophical Tale

During the first year of *Der Wandsbecker Bote* there appeared a piece which was later included in *Asmus I–II* under the title *"Eine Chria,* darin ich von meinem akademischen Leben und Wandel Nachricht gebe" [*A Chria,* in which I give an account of my academic life].[13] The work is a short dramatic narrative in which Asmus relates his visit together with a group of students to a university lecture on philosophy as well as his response to the experience.

Asmus sets the scene briefly, describing the students sitting on benches as if they were in church. A professor, "or something or other," is seated on a footstool, holding speeches on this and that, which is called "lecturing."[14] The students have indicated that his learning is even greater and kinkier than his wig. Asmus feels there must be something to this, "for he ran on as if it were coming from a cider filling hose; and he could demonstrate like the wind. Whenever he'd undertake something, he'd begin just a little, and, before you could turn around, it was demonstrated."[15]

Asmus then gives a couple of examples of the professor's method: "Thus, he demonstrated, e.g., that a student's a student and not a rhinoceros. Then he said a student's either a student or a rhinoceros. But now, a student's not a rhinoceros, because otherwise a rhinoceros'd have to be a student, too. But a rhinoceros isn't a student; thus, a student's a student."[16] This "thing" about a student and a rhinoceros, the professor said, is a main support of all philosophy, and he and his colleagues cannot put their backs to it firmly enough to keep it from falling over. The professor then spoke of another support, actually of more than one. There was one designed for everybody and another only for him and his colleagues, which requires a finer nose: "As when a spider spins a thread, the thread is for everyone and everyone for the thread. But at the hindmost part of the spider there is its modest part, namely the *other* something, which is the sufficient reason for the *first* something, and each something must have such a sufficient reason, but it need not always be in the hindmost part."[17] Everything in philosophy is ruined if this is missing.

Subsequently, the professor took the field against the ignorant: "Man alive, how he raked them over the coals! The prejudices of nightmares, corns, and religion, etc., light on the unlearned mob like flies on the nose and sting them. But none may approach him, the Master of Arts, and if one did, whop!, he'd smack it dead on his nose with the swatter of philosophy."[18] The professor goes on to say that only philosophy can teach whether God exists and what he is; without it, no one can have any conception of him. Asmus feels the professor was just saying that. No one can accuse him of being a philosopher, yet, "I never walk through a forest but what it occurs to me who makes the trees grow, and then I sense something, faintly and from far away, of a stranger, and I'd bet I'm thinking of God then, I shiver so with reverence and joy."[19]

The professor continued to talk about everything as if he had helped to make it all. To Asmus, however, he did not seem as wise as Solomon: "I think that anyone who *really* knows something has to, has to—if I saw one just once I bet I'd recognize him. I'd paint him, too, with a bright, cheerful, peaceful expression, with a quiet, great conviction, etc. Such a person can't show off, least of all despise others and rake them over the coals."[20] Asmus ends his account by reflecting, "Oh! Conceit, and pride is an unfriendly passion. Grass and flowers can't thrive near them."[21]

The word *chria* designates a systematic treatment of a philosophical or literary statement or fact which had been used as a rhetorical exercise since antiquity. In retrospect there is a contradiction between the pompous title and both Asmus and his narration, which manifests itself most emphatically in Asmus's language and as early as the first sentences: "Bin auch auf Unverstädten gewesen, und hab auch studiert. Ne, studiert hab ich nicht, aber auf Unverstädten bin ich gewesen, und weiβ von allem Bescheid" ("I went to the university, too, and studied, myself. Na-a, I didn't really study, but I went to the university and know all about it").[22] Here, Asmus mixes *Universität* ("university") and *Unverstand* ("ignorance," "stupidity") in the untranslatable word *Unverstädten.* This involuntarily revealing confusion and the highly colloquial language in which it appears immediately place Asmus and his account in a peculiar light.

This light grows brighter the longer Asmus speaks. His homespun idiom continually clashes with the situation described, and his nature imagery is out of place in the halls of learning. No less so is his language of feeling, his shivering in the forest and his initial, emotion-filled inability to describe a truly wise man, which leads to a breach in syntax. There is also an illuminating contradiction between the title and the real *chria*—the professor's comparison between a student and a rhinoceros and the scatological implications of his discussion of the spider—which is also involuntarily revealing and which Asmus does not perceive.

Asmus need not imply that the insights provided by the principles of identity and contradiction and sufficient reason, both foundations of rationalistic methodology, are self-evident. He need not suggest that the professor is not as wise as Solomon. The contrast between his language and syntax and the aridly intellectual, self-compromising character of the lecture tells us all we need to know. Through his naiveté and immediate, natural response to the situation he discloses the artificiality and inadequacy of the professor and his discipline and reveals himself to be far wiser than the highly educated academic. He indeed "knows all about it."

Asmus is an early, full-blown example of the ingenue, a figure who appears in numerous guises throughout Claudius's work. In developing the figure, at base a variation of the wise fool, Claudius entered a tradition which extended from Plato's Socratic dialogues through Shakespeare's jesters to Henry Fielding's Parson Adams, Laurence Sterne's Uncle Toby, and many others during his own time. The ingenue allowed Claudius to comment humorously and indirectly on his subject matter, here, to counter the unnaturalness and presumption of school philosophy and theology and their representatives with the truth of the heart. From this confrontation emerge his view of the intuitive nature of religious experience and the role of colloquial language in expressing it as well as his Socratic approach to life.

The obliqueness of statement derives ultimately from the formal possibilities furnished by the ingenue. The figure enables Claudius to distance both himself and his reader from the ostensible subject matter, the professor's lecture—to create another subjective, but at the same time broader, perspective on it. The perspectives of the professor and Asmus run parallel to each other throughout the work and thus supply its unifying structural principle. Moreover, they jar with each other at every step of the way, creating a simple form of irony in which the opposite of what is asserted proves to be true. The total message of the work and its satiric character emerge from a comparison of these perspectives.

A Letter to a Friend in South America

Since antiquity, the fictitious literary epistle had been employed both for serious philosophical and literary discussion and for satirical purposes, the latter, indeed, made possible by the former. Claudius utilized the form extensively and variously during his entire career. It proved to be, in fact, his major prose genre and represents another point of close contact with literary tradition. In his *Schreiben an einen Freund am Fluß Essequebo* [Letter to a friend on the River Essiquebo], published in the *Adreß-Comptoir-Nachrichten,* he gives an early demonstration of his command of one possibility of the form.[23]

The fictitious correspondent approaches his friend in faraway Guiana formally—"Sir!"—in the tone of one interested in enlightening his friend on an unfamiliar, at once serious and difficult matter. He introduces the subject by providing a concrete example:

> As often as it occurs to you to place your black foot on the surface of your good river, be it by sunlight, or moonlight, or no light at all, you will notice that a different phenomenon occurs than when you place it upon the earth and that your foot, knee, etc., etc., after you have made your resolution, gradually become invisible. Here in our country it is different. There are certain times when the surface of our river is hard and when we people stand on the middle of the river and dance about magically over the waters. During your study of such a water spirit you would, if you were here, come upon two steel amulets, which he has beneath the soles of his feet, and to all appearances seek in them the entire magic power, which nevertheless lies only in part in them.[24]

After this long introduction it becomes apparent that the subject of his discourse is the ice skate.

The correspondent then launches into a discussion of the problematic nature of the terms *Schrittschuh* and *Schlittschuh,* both of which are used to designate the object under consideration. So problematic is it, indeed, that he finds it necessary to treat the etymology of the word *Schrittschuh* in greater detail. He first casts a glance at the development of means of traversing snow and frozen waters in the northern countries. Subsequently, he cites Diomedes in the ancient Greek, introduces old Norse terms with original and translated commentary by old Scandinavian scholars, and offers the modern Danish and German equivalents—all in an attempt to present the older *Schrittschuh* as the historically legitimate word. He closes by writing, "You will have noticed what I am leading to. However, I advise you not to think of a certain verse by Horace, which begins with 'Oh-.' Achilles deserved an Iliad for it nonetheless, even though Hercules was his predecessor in great deeds."[25]

The fact that the contemporary etymologist would disagree with our scholar's exposition of the origins of the two words will likely not concern the modern reader greatly.[26] For the work is a delightful parody of the rationalistic philosophical treatise and the attitude toward life from which it proceeds. The pompous, precious tone of much academic writing and the arsenal of philosophical methodology are placed here in the service of an altogether negligible subject. The writer's approach and the philosophical treatise as a quite familiar genre form perspectives which stand in ironic contrast to that of the innocuous matter under consideration. As in *Eine Chria,* this discrepancy yields both the satirical commentary and the structure of the work. Unlike *Eine Chria,* however, the present professorial figure has the word from beginning to end. His point of view predominates, his friend remaining an entirely silent addressee. Consequently, the perspectivism is more indirect and the irony more implicit than in the narrative.

Yet, the authorial distance nevertheless created by the figure allowed Claudius to contrive, as it were, the self-destruction of the treatise and to land a final satiric coup. The scholar's allusion at the end of the piece seems to refer to the first poem in Book III of Horace's odes and epodes, which begins,

> I scorn the secular crowd and keep them out.
> Be silent. I am a priest of the Muses
>   and I chant for young men and maidens
>   poems that have never been heard before.[27]

By admonishing his friend to disregard this priest's claim to precedence and invoking Achilles in self-defense, our academic concedes, in characteristic style, the existence of a precursor and rather overzealously attempts to conceal the superfluity of his enterprise.

The allusion makes complete and most delightful sense, however, only if one looks beyond the text itself. Claudius's friend Klopstock not only excelled on the ice but preached the gospel of his favorite pastime as well. As Goethe reminisces in *Dichtung und Wahrheit,* the older poet was well versed in all matters related to the sport, including the history of its terminology, and pleaded loudly to all who would listen for a return to—the old word *Schrittschuh.*[28] The scholarly reference to Horace and Greek mythology thus represents Claudius's witty and oblique homage to Klopstock's zeal and playful appeal for recognition of his own endeavors in behalf of the *cause célèbre.* For the initiated in Hamburg and Copenhagen this final, personal note must have robbed the scholar of any remaining credibility and heightened the already abundant irony of a satire successful in itself. Claudius parodied the philosophical treatise in similar epistolary fashion in a number of his early works. However, he produced equally compelling and perhaps even more characteristic parodies in another approach to the form.

Two Cousins

One of the many correspondences between Asmus and *Vetter* first appeared in 1778 in the *Deutsches Museum* and later in the year in Book III of the collected works under the title *"Eine Korrespondenz zwischen mir und meinem Vetter,* das Studium der schönen Wissenschaften betreffend" [A Correspondence between me and my cousin concerning the study of the fine arts].[29] In the first of two letters Asmus expresses interest in the fine arts, especially literature, and asks his cousin where he should begin his study. The second contains *Vetter*'s reply.

Asmus addresses *Vetter,* "Most Learned, Most Revered Cousin." He wants to "take up" the arts, "so that whenever a poem or a prose [*sic*] stirs in my heart and wants out on this or that occasion I could give the thing a fine, finished appearance and *grazias,* as they say."[30] He then requests *Vetter*'s advice and a list of helpful books. He remembers the French theorist Charles Batteux from his schooldays with Rector Ahrens but feels that new modes have surely appeared since then: "The latest, Cousin well knows, is after all always the best, and one hates to show up in a pointed wig when hair bags are hanging at every neck."[31] In the next breath he adds, "Cousin will receive the horseradish next week from Grumpenhagen, the wagoner," and then closes, "wherewith I have the honor of remaining My Most Learned and Most Revered Cousin's Obedient Servant and Cousin, Asmus."[32]

Vetter answers as follows:

> Don't be a fool, Cousin, and leave the fine arts be. But I won't keep my advice from you.
>
> 1) If you're really serious about this or that, and it gets you to the quick, then let it get you, and thank God for it, and say nothing to anyone about it; and
> 2) If it's useful to make it known and to write, then write away what and how you feel.
> 3) But if you feel nothing and would still like to give the learned public the impression, then read Batteux and his colleagues from Longinus to the one who pisses on the wall and in the newspapers and journals. You can leave them unread, too, for you write nothing but foolish stuff in verse and prose.[33]

In a footnote he adds, "You can also grind the horseradish instead of Batteux, it all amounts to the same thing."[34]

This exchange of brief letters represents another formal variation of Claudius's response to the contemporary rationalization of life, here in the form of normative-systematic poetics. Asmus solicits *Vetter*'s assistance in a mixture of colloquial language and learned phraseology and jargon which is itself inconsistent and entirely inappropriate in what is, after all, a familiar letter. Moreover, the whole tenor of his letter contradicts his more characteristic sobriety in such questions, which lends his approach to the matter a certain eye-winking roguishness. *Vetter* participates in the game by responding formally in a scholarly manner, his advice carefully "systematized" in three tidy sections. However, the nature of his advice and his straightforward, colloquial, and in one passage vulgar language contrast starkly with the learned form of presentation.

Thus a number of ironies and, accordingly, points of view run through the short piece. On the one hand there is Asmus's dissembling posture, his street-corner and lecture-hall style, and the "informality" of his letter. Through their interplay they humorously disqualify the attitude toward the arts ostensibly represented and imply quite another. As if this were not enough, there are, on the other hand, *Vetter*'s complicity in the sport, his scholarly style, and candid, colorful language. Asmus's sudden introduction of the completely unrelated and banal horseradish and *Vetter*'s not unexpected return to it serve as another self-destructive device. A healthy portion of Claudius is contained in this recurring ploy.

The work is an early and pregnant expression of Claudius's views of knowledge, language, and poetics. He asserts here the primacy of intuitive experience and the virtue of silence as well as the role of natural language and the falseness of the attempt to embrace life and truth through the intellect alone. Moreover, the piece exemplifies his characteristic tendency to split himself into separate identities and further to refract their perspectives in his approach to theme and structure. In this and many other works he goes beyond the points of view of the narrator and single correspondent as discussed thus far, gaining a freer hand in the process, and finds one of his most congenial prose forms.

A New Year's Greeting

Claudius introduced the second volume of the *Adreβ-Comptoir-Nachrichten* with a feuilletonistic piece which may well have made the reader first wrinkle his brow, then smile, and finally, perhaps, think. Later given the title *Zum 1. Januar 1770* {On January 1st, 1770}, the work appears initially to be a commentary on the passing of the old year and the coming of the new like many another.[35] However, further reading reveals a quite different, if in part familiar, theme and a partly novel stylistic approach to it:

When thinking of the years, it is quite remarkable and pleasant how one always comes after the other and attaches itself so accurately that one never perceives an empty space between them. One can picture this very nicely in the image of a snake, which has its tail in its mouth, or in the image of a wheel, too, on which a criminal is bound, and I myself would prefer the wheel, if it were not dishonest. For are we men not, as it were, bound by the hand of fate to the wheel of the year? To be sure, the proverb of the Latins, omne simile claudicat, in German, every simile has a short foot, applies here, too, but for that reason the custom of writing verses on the end and beginning of the year is still very praiseworthy, and one wonders whether one should not do too much rather than too little of it. One can, of course, also use prose on this occasion, for why should someone refrain who does not have the gift of mellifluous poetry, although one cannot deny that poetic words, especially the spondee, are more appropriate here, because it consists of two long feet, just as the years are all the same, namely three hundred sixty-five days. Now, one could of course object and say that the days of the year are dactylic, or now short, now long, and that, consequently, a competentia of these two verse forms occurs, but because the Copernican system is entirely accepted by almost all scholars and one must consider both the state of nutrition and decorum in a well-organized republic, many have therefore assumed with good reason that prosaic essays, which, according to the verse form of the state of nutrition and the comparison of a well-organized republic, in addition to the competence of the spondee and dactyl at the end of the year, no less than the decorum which the Romans used to observe, when they were bound to the wheel, by no means in the absence of something better, the image of a snake, which has its tail in its mouth, and the accuracy of the Copernican system --[36]

If the work grows increasingly confusing the more one reads, this confusion is, on careful inspection, highly calculated. It quickly becomes clear that the piece is more than a conventional New Year's greeting. The writer rummages about in the paraphernalia of learning—illustrative images and comparisons, a Latin word here and a

Latin proverb together with translation there—and places them in a meandering line of argumentation which merely explains the natural passage of time and justifies the harmless practice of commemorating it in literary fashion. He presents not a New Year's greeting as such, but rather a "study" and "defense" of the form. He thus seems at the outset to be bent on parodying the philosophical treatise in the manner of our expert on ice-skating, after all.

However, the second impression proves to be as deceptive as the first, for something new begins to happen several lines into the work. The writer says that he would prefer the image of the wheel if it were not dishonest. Proceeding from this last statement, the conjunction "for," which introduces the next sentence, leads one to expect some explanation of the "dishonesty" of the image. What follows, instead, is an affirmation of the felicity of the figure. The adverb "to be sure," which begins the ensuing sentence, concedes the impotency of imagery to capture the full significance of its objects. Yet, the adverb "for that reason," with which the second clause sets in, appears to make this powerlessness itself the reason for writing such verses and for using poetic language after all. The writer's argumentation turns out to be rather loose and inconsistent. The connecting words create an uneasy amplificatory or causal relationship between the sentences and clauses they introduce, which complements the far-fetched and inappropriate nature of the learned comparisons themselves.

This sense of uneasiness increases drastically toward the end of the piece. Roughly the last third is comprised of a single sentence containing over 115 words and a myriad of clauses. The writer's exposition continues to wind its serpentine way for a space. However, its contents—the plasticity of the dactyl as an image, the Copernican system, the well-organized republic, etc.—gradually lose any contextual relationship to each other, bound together only by grammatical connections. Moreover, the clauses beginning with "that prosaic essays" have no governing predicate and lack even a grammatical relationship. They simply stand in a row with no logical coherence and, it should be added, with no end. The result is something resembling double talk.

The first two-thirds of the work are structured generally on the telling discrepancy between style and content observed earlier. In its simplest form, exemplified here, the resulting irony makes its statement merely by imposing two essentially unrelated areas of experience upon the language, as it were, from without and by requiring a comparison of the two. By then allowing the writer's scholarly argumentation to degenerate into nonsense, however, Claudius permits his medium to become its own statement through its very nature. A comparison of disparate perspectives is no longer necessary, for the language generates an adequate and organic point of view itself. This New Year's greeting is thus only in part a traditional parody of the philosophical treatise and all it stands for. By drawing the poetic medium into its pale as well and manifesting its innate powerlessness to extract positive sense from either, it becomes an unconventional satire of all language and its inability to convey truth. The piece represents Claudius's early pessimism toward language and an inchoate attitude toward an entirely different order of satiric language and thus warrants attention.

If we have devoted a considerable portion of our relatively brief study to Claudius's satire, it is in part because this mode of expression is highly characteristic, although not all-inclusive, of his approach to prose and certain major themes, especially during his youth. Another reason is the feeling that Claudius's satire deserves more attention than it has so far received. It is often more subtly modulated, complex, and witty than that of accepted satirists such as Gottlieb Wilhelm Rabener and Christian Ludwig Liscow and in a few works such as the one just discussed points toward a new satire.[37] A more thorough comparison of Claudius's satire with that of such writers might reveal another star in a not particularly lustrous firmament in German literature.

Asmus Writes to Andres

Despite the fact that he never appears in print, Andres remained Asmus's favorite and most constant correspondent. Over the years Asmus wrote some thirty-four letters to him and in them opened his heart on most of his closest concerns. In one of his early letters he discloses still another approach to one of these and to the epistolary form as well.

In this *Brief an Andres* Asmus informs his friend that the evening star along with the moon and Jupiter will be especially visible in a couple of evenings.[38] He sympathizes with Andres's having forgotten his astronomy, which his old schoolmate had apparently lamented in an earlier letter. He recalls that Andres had had a difficult time understanding Rector Ahrens's instruction in geometry. Ahrens knew everything by heart, while Andres could comprehend nothing. Yet, "you, even in your simplicity, could look at a bright star for a whole half hour and be so happy about it inside, and Herr Ahrens couldn't do that, and that's why I liked you more."[39] Asmus then says that Herr Ahrens can demonstrate the secrets of the heavenly bodies all he likes. Andres, though, should go outside and look at the moon and the stars: "and what goes through your mind as you're standing there in your doorway and looking out, Andres, well, your old school pal wishes you that, and Herr Ahrens knows nothing about it. Farewell, Andres, and don't forget to bolt the door when you go back inside."[40]

This short piece contains stylistic features common to other epistles but in a quite new constellation and with an entirely different effect. First of all, three distinct personalities with individual points of view appear. In his naiveté and ignorance Andres embodies salient characteristics of the ingenue as encountered in other figures. However, his sensibility lends him an emotional depth foreign to most of them. Rector Ahrens, on the other hand, has the exclusively rational grasp on life typical of most of Claudius's academics. Asmus, in turn, combines something of Ahrens's understanding with Andres's immediate emotional responsiveness, standing and mediating between them. His broader perspective illuminates the more limited ones of Andres and Ahrens and their relationship to each other. In part by playing these three foils against each other, Claudius allows the supremacy of the intuitive experience of life to emerge as a simple matter of fact.

This self-evidence derives, however, as much from the timbre of Asmus's conversational tone as from the structure of his letter. Throughout, he himself maintains a level of feeling which makes any irony or satire absolutely superfluous. His concern for Andres's safety, expressed unexpectedly in the final sentence, which calls to mind a certain delivery of horseradish, is pure Asmus—and pure Claudius as well. In this piece Claudius asserts his view in a serious and positive manner and offers another variation of one of his most congenial prose forms.

A Fit of Philosophy

During his long career Claudius suffered many attacks by the goddess of wisdom but gave only three of their literary results the appropriate title, *Impetus philosophicus.*[41] In the earliest one, published in *Der Wandsbecker Bote* in 1772, he responded in a fashion not as yet encountered in our review of his prose.

Alles hat seine Zeit, Schreiben und Rezensieren, und unwillig sein und brummen auch, daβ alles das wenig frommet, und den hungrigen Wolf nicht sättigt, der in mir nach Wahrheit und Wissen bellt, und wütet–wie eine Wölfin der ihre Jungen geraubt sind, denn ich hatte einst eine Faust voll Sonnenstrahlen mit den Wurzeln und Fasern, und sahe wie sie hervorwachsen, bin einst hinterm Mond gestanden und wuβte das Geheimnis der Verwesung–und des Genies von oben her, aber geraubt ist mir's bis auf leichte Narben und Ahndungen, als mir der Rock von Fellen angetan ward. Der Weg, leise Ahndungen in lauten Ausruf zu verwandeln–ein leichter ätherischer Jüngling zu werden der in den Tälern und Höhen der Schöpfung überall frei lustwandelt und die Leiter Jakobs hinauf- und herabsteigen kann–geht nicht über Barbara celarent, und ist wenigen recht bekannt—Und ich sahe an alles was geschrieben und rezensiert wird–und, siehe, es war alles eitel, und neben der guten Göttin die eine volle Meβurne ausgoβ sah ich einen gähnenden Knaben.[42]

There is a season for all things, writing and reviewing, and being angry and grumbling, too, that it is all of little use and does not sate the hungry wolf in me baying for truth and knowledge and raging–like a she-wolf whose young have been stolen from her, for I once had a fistful of sunbeams with the roots and threads and saw how they grow forth, once stood beyond the moon and knew the secret of decay–and of the spirit from above, but it was stolen from me down to light scars and intimations when the coat of fur was cast upon me. The way to transform faint intimations into a loud cry–to become a light, ethereal youth, who wanders freely over the valleys and heights of creation and can climb up and down Jacob's ladder–does not pass by barbara celarent and is known well to few—And I looked at all that is written and reviewed–and, behold, it was all vain, and next to the good goddess pouring out a full urn I saw a yawning boy.

The highly allusive and figurative language of this piece and the loose syntactical structures in which it is couched might well lead one to designate the resultant style as a kind of poetic prose. Certainly, it seems to contrast vividly with that of the works considered up to this point and indeed does so to a significant extent. Yet, there are similarities as well.

The almost word-for-word reproduction of the first line of the famous third chapter of Ecclesiastes at the outset immediately lends the work a frame of reference which extends from the eternal-universal to the temporal-particular. At the same time the deep pessimism toward earthly life expressed by the Old Testament author, said to have been the wise Solomon, suggestively colors the mood of the present writer, sitting in his study and reflecting on the value of his endeavors. Indeed, the ancient author himself places book writing and studying in question. Our writer's sense of dignity, but also of earthboundness and futility is accentuated by his metaphorical description of himself as an animal, a wolf—noble and beautiful but at the same time alone in the vast, nocturnal landscape evoked by the image. His feeling of essential loss is poignantly objectified in the related simile of a mother wolf bereft of her young.

The free metaphorical leap in the next phrase illustrates the reason for this sense of uselessness and isolation. The image of sunrays, suggestive within the cosmos of the work of absolute truth, is mixed synaesthetically with that of roots with their threads and plant growth, elements of the vegetable world. Their combination, possible only in poetic imagery, implies an organic relationship between the realms of spirit and matter. The writer, clutching these unique beams in his hand, thus once possessed perfect knowledge. This idea is varied and broadened in the following phrase with its associative shift to the moon and organic decay and the genius on high. Transported poetically through time and space, the writer had direct access not only to truth but to its originator as well. The key words here are "once" and "had," for the writer, who in the meantime has come to stand for all men, has lost this possession. This is emphasized by the metaphorical return to the temporal world, represented by light scars and intimations—physical and spiritual healed wounds—which are all that remain. The writer's and man's present this-sidedness is heightened by the image of the cloak of fur, which calls the animal kingdom and the wolves back to mind.

The next sentence expands on the circumstances of man's trammeled existence. Like the idealized youth who can traverse all creation and even climb Jacob's ladder, there are those who retain the ability to overcome the gap separating them from the realm of spirit and to express the knowledge gained from the source. Their numbers are few, however, and their ability does not derive from the temporal, apparently often belabored intellect, represented by *barbara celarent* (see note 42). The first part of the final phrase, beginning with "And I looked at" and ending with "and, behold, it was all vain," completes a full swing back to the language and pessimism of the Old Testament author, who uses these expressions throughout his reflections. While the figures of the goddess and boy at the end resist an entirely satisfactory explanation, they seem to vary the basic theme of man's inability to grasp absolute knowledge, which exists nonetheless, and the senselessness of his activity. Moreover, they lead beyond the Judeo-Christian world to that of classical antiquity and suggest that even the greatest period of endeavor in human history found no solution to the problem.

There is thus a circular movement within the work, borne in part by the imagery. The allusions and figures create a cosmos structured by two poles, the spiritual and phenomenal, and alternate back and forth between the two, showing their original, essential relationship and its loss. These devices, which evoke the realm of space and eternity and the animal and plant kingdoms, the biblical world and that of learning and classical antiquity, provide various perspectives on this relationship from within the cosmos of the work.

The inner logic of the imagery is complemented by that of the structure of the piece. Despite the initial impression, the work is quite argumentative in character. The first sentence presents a thesis through the image of the baying wolf: while writing and reviewing have their time, they are ultimately of little avail in the search for and expression of truth. The remainder of this sentence and the next one, ending with "known well to few," explain and illustrate this thesis: writing and reviewing are of little use because of man's loss of direct access to truth due to his phenomenality. The remainder of the piece simply reasserts and illustrates the original thesis. Thus, the work has a closed circular structure based on the progression from tenet to explanation-illustration to tenet, now more clearly demonstrated and perceived.

This quite rational structure is concealed, in part, by the syntactical patterns in which it is cast. First of all, fully 170 words appear in two, or perhaps three, extremely long sentences. The sentence length and the numerous, varied clauses prevent a succinct development and perception of the thought content; the arrangement of the clauses has the same effect. Such syntax cannot convey sober, rational discourse.

Of course, it was not intended to. The rational structure of the piece is hidden by the highly associative, emotive language as well as the loose syntax. The emotional and rational elements of the work enter into an inseparable union, in which each has an equally valid *raison d'être.* The piece is designed to compel the reader to a living understanding of its content through an appeal both to the feelings and the intellect. The view of the separation of the realms of spirit and matter and the inadequacy of language and reason to reunite them is a matter accessible to both. Claudius thus finds here a form corresponding to the nature of his theme and his addressee.

This work will have to stand for many in which Claudius employs poetic prose. He almost never uses such language for strictly emotive purposes or as an aesthetic game, but virtually always within an at least implicitly rational context and for partly rationalistic purposes. The piece is thus important not only as an example of a characteristic, early usage of the prose medium and as an expression of his pessimism regarding language and knowledge where ultimates are concerned. It is also an indication of the role of language and intellect within their proper domain and of another point of contact between Claudius and his rationalistic age.

A Youth Sees His First Plays

On 8 November 1769, the famous company of actors led by Konrad Ernst Ackermann presented a performance of *Minna von Barnhelm* which exceeded even Lessing's own expectations; on the first evening of December of the same year they brought Weiße's *Romeo und Julia* to life once again.[43] Claudius was present both times and offered his impressions and something more in three issues of the *Adreß-Comptoir-Nachrichten.*[44] The *Korrespondenz zwischen Fritz, seinem Vater und seiner Tante* [Correspondence among Fritz, his father, and his aunt], as it was later called, is a *unicum* of dramatic criticism, which places Claudius's poetics into an entirely different light and further illuminates his treatment of the epistolary form as well.[45]

The work consists of an introduction by a fictional editor and five letters, three from Fritz to his father and one each from his father and aunt to him. The editor opens his prefatory remarks by referring to a friend's comparison of a well-performed play to a sharply loaded cannon: "Not the report which rolls through the entire countryside, not the forest nor the gleaming palaces which echo it; the split oak tree, the torn mountainside, prove that the cannon was sharply loaded."[46] He then mentions the presence of a naive, ignorant youth at a performance of *Minna von Barnhelm* and his letter to his father: "It is to be sure only the letter of an ignorant youth, but still just as good as the report of shallow encomia, even if the walls of the most beautiful palace had echoed it."[47]

In his first letter Fritz writes initially of his arrival in Hamburg and wonder at the "big city," seen from the side of his cousin. He then recounts how his cousin took him to a "music house" one evening, where around a thousand people were sitting on benches or in book repositories hanging one over the other on the walls. Subsequently, he relates the events which took place in the inn unexpectedly revealed behind the curtain, all in colorful confusion: "Some travelers who knew and were looking for each other and were staying at the same inn without knowing it found each other. That was a commotion, there were joy and sorrow and quarreling, and joy again and quarreling and love again, and friendship and generosity, all mixed up."[48] His description of the people involved is no less colorful: "There was a pretty widow, who was more sorrowful than she looked, a chambermaid who looked more mischievous than she was, an excellent sergeant, a fellow who had money, and a slender young lady I could have done anything in the world for–yes, but Major von Tellheim acted as an upright man by her."[49] In the same unaffected manner Fritz then relates the particulars of the conflict, intrigue, and happy ending.

If Fritz is unable to render a systematic plot summary and character study, he has no difficulty in expressing his own response to the experience and that of the other spectators: "But they must have been a really good sort of people. People at home aren't like that; there must not be many like that here either, because everybody in the hall was astonished by them, stared at them with eyes and ears, and forgot all about everything else because of them. . . . Oh! I can't really tell you how it all was. But I'm not your Fritz if what these people said and did didn't bring tears to my eyes three times."[50] Fritz writes that he has learned that a man named Lessing made up the whole story: "Well, may God forgive him for giving the major and the poor lady such a hard time. I sure won't tip my hat to him if he meets me. But I'd give ten silver dollars if I could see such a story again. The whole evening my heart was so big and so warm–I had such a hot thirst for noble deeds–yes, I really believe that if you saw such people often you could finally become upright and big-hearted along with them yourself."[51]

In his reply Fritz's father expresses approval of his son's immediate response to the play, for "The gods gave man a heart which can surge upward and with the warmer blood can bring soft color to his face, tears to his eyes, and with them a sensation of bliss and an irresistibly sweet feeling of joy through his smallest nerves. . . ."[52] However, he goes on to say that the gods also gave man common sense to control these surges and to lead to his true well-being. Too great a reliance on the feelings makes man unhappy. Not everyone acts as nobly as the people in the play, and Fritz should be on guard against them. He closes by saying that Fritz can always tip his hat to Lessing.

Fritz's aunt, on the other hand, is not so edified by her nephew's letter. In her answer she shakes her finger at him: "And you're not ashamed to boast in your letter about a retired sergeant and a young lady you saw! I thank God on my knees for not giving me any children or a husband, so that I don't have to witness such sin and shame in my own offspring. Fie on you, and don't ever let me see you again."[53]

In his second letter to his father Fritz writes of his subsequent return to the theater, where he saw the young lady again but without the sergeant and Tellheim. He expresses amazement that the men could abandon her, unaware that the actress is in a different role. He then includes his aunt's letter and says of it, "She calls me a secret scape goat, and that she'll have to prove. And even if a pure seraph were always standing visibly next to me, I'd to be sure bend my knee before him every hour, but I'd look him freely in the face with all I thought and did and would do and think no more or less than right now."[54] Afterwards, Fritz thanks his father for his advice in even more enthusiastic language and he promises to heed it.

Fritz's reaction to *Romeo und Julia,* described in his final letter, is much like his response to Lessing's play. After bemoaning the death of Minna in this work, again confusing dramatic illusion and reality, he expresses his joy on learning that everyone is still alive after all and that it was all a comedy. Not sure just what that is, he says that he will inquire further into the matter.

Even more so than the narrator of *Eine Chria,* Fritz is the ingenue par excellence; and here as well as there this is not at all a liability. Precisely because of his naiveté he responds to dramatic art naturally, which is to say with emotional immediacy and without reflection. Due to this directness, as evident in the confusion of his impressions and his exuberant language, he and the other spectators are led by the noble action on stage to an enthusiastic desire to act nobly themselves. He is at once entertained and guided to truth by the handling of an art form which addresses his primary faculty for entertainment and the perception of truth. Indeed, he is the split oak tree and the torn mountainside mentioned in the introduction to the work.

Fritz's limited but most valid perspective is affirmed by the broader points of view of the editor and his acquaintance, who are conditioned by greater experience and knowledge of the world. The editor is, after all, impressed enough by the truth of the ignorant youth's letters to recall his acquaintance's comparison and to present the correspondence to the public. Fritz's father approves of his son's reaction to the play for the same reasons and from the same broader perspective. However, he adds a new and complementary perspective by impressing on his son the role of common sense in directing the truth gained through emotional experience. The measured and reflective, yet warm and in part imagistic language of both the editor and the father corresponds to the nature of their statements. Fritz's aunt presents a common but far more limited perspective on the matter. Her exaggerated indignation, Fritz's reply, and his experience itself all serve to qualify her view seriously. Indeed, she perhaps exemplifies the truth of her brother's admonition concerning the role of common sense in guiding the emotions. She also represents the concerns of Goeze and others who criticized the theater on the basis of its alleged immorality.

Despite Fritz's lack of method Lessing had reason to be pleased with the reception given him in Claudius's work. Fritz's descriptions of the plot and characters of *Minna von Barnhelm* are penetrating in all their effervescence, and he does not entirely overlook their tragic potential.[55] The differentiation and both implicit and explicit recognition offered by the interplay of the other characters could have been nothing less than flattering to the author.

The work is a piece of dramatic and literary criticism which in its formal originality goes beyond the pale of both contemporary commentary and Claudius's other reviews. At the same time it gives a more positive and balanced picture of Claudius's views on poetics and epistemology, revealing an entirely different mood than that of *Impetus philosophicus,* from which it is separated by only three and a half years. Finally, the work represents one of Claudius's most concerted efforts to arrive at truth by illuminating a subject from various sides, both within a text and through the relationship between text and fictional framework. It is thus one of Claudius's most characteristic and successful treatments of the epistolary form and the prose medium.

Chapter Four

The Poetry: Correction and Revelation

A glance at the publication dates of significant and mature works of poetry written during the eighteenth century indicates that the 1760s represented something of a hiatus in the development of the genre.[1] In view of this general lack of direction it is small wonder that the poetry of the emerging Claudius exhibits a certain formal and thematic incoherence, often amounting to contradiction, and that these features are observable even after he found himself toward the end of the decade. A number of the aphorisms, the *Tändeleien und Erzählungen,* the letters to the moon, and similar works pay homage to the past, while many others criticize it. Due in part perhaps to dissatisfaction with the possibilities offered by his age, Claudius looked to the folk song, the Protestant hymn, and the Bible for inspiration. In any event his critical assimilation of varied traditions eventually culminated in a highly personal poetic art. Indeed, his achievement lies not so much in innovation per se as in innovative usage of tradition.

Considering the small body of his verse and the prevailing view of its uniform simplicity and piety, Claudius's poetry appears surprisingly rich in form and motif. In addition to the folk song and Protestant hymn he drew upon genres as varied as the fable and the cantata, the verse narrative and the epigram, the romance and other song forms. His prosody displays certain constants but great variation as well. A survey of the poetry reveals that he generally favored a short folk-song form, that is, a poem consisting of one to a few quatrains of alternating iambic tetrameter and trimeter lines with a rhyme scheme of *a b a b.* Almost half of the poems consist of a single strophe, and nearly a fourth of the remainder contain but two or three, which suggests a parallel to the brevity of the prose.

However, this is as it were an ideal type. Another fourth of the pieces of more than one strophe range from ten to as many as thirty-four stanzas. The quatrain is by far the most common single strophic form, the couplet and sestet following at a remote distance; yet, strophes with varying line counts are more numerous than any of these. While the iamb is far and away the predominant foot, there are a number of works with trochaic meter, including a few folk songs, and an almost equally great number with irregularly mixed feet. If one encounters the tetrameter more often than any other line, regular mixtures and, to an even greater extent, irregular mixtures of line lengths are the rule. The poems are almost invariably rhymed, which reflects a belief in the importance of musicality. Yet, even here the prevalent tendency is complemented by an almost equal inclination toward variation, in the form of other regularly alternating schemes, e.g., *a b b a,* and of irregular mixtures. And in at least nine pieces rhyme is not employed at all.

Claudius's poetry does not abound with the poetic figures which one has perhaps come to expect since Classicism and Romanticism. However, imagery is abundant, varied, and employed in a highly personal way. Claudius's usage of personification and allusion is also rich and equally individualistic. His syntax often plays a decisive role in the total statement of a work. He at times manifests an acute sense of the thematic possibilities of the acoustic dimension of poetry beyond end rhyme.

All the major themes discussed in Chapter 2 appear in the poetry as well as in the prose. It will come as no surprise that religion is predominant and that those poems which are related to most intimately personal experience, e.g., family and death, are among the most common. What may be surprising is the fact that sociopolitical themes are more frequent in the verse than in the prose, second only to religion, and that art follows close behind, assuming almost as much relative importance as in the prose.

Given the variation of tone, subject matter, and form within a basic general framework, one might characterize Claudius's poetry by reversing the terms of the concept expressed in Goethe's poem "Dauer im Wechsel" [Constancy in change]. Claudius evinces as little respect for the pure genre in his verse as in his prose and in perhaps most instances creates his own *genres mêlés* here as well as there.

While emphasizing the often overlooked variety in Claudius's poetry, one must also acknowledge the presence of important invariables. For they are equally typical of his verse and, moreover, frequently indicate the close connection between the poetry and the prose. The personae of the poems, although possessing somewhat more limited possibilities, are essentially those of the epistles and dialogues. The implied reader and the relationship between persona and reader are basically the same. Indeed, the poetry manifests much the same dialogical character and perspectivism as the prose. Most significantly, the view and usage of language as an expression of an attitude toward life and its manifold concerns are identical to those of the prose. These and other uniform features thus suggest the unity of the entire work.

Claudius's poems embody these characteristics in different ways and to different extents. Many do not reflect them at all, being quite conventional and therefore perhaps less interesting than others. Some are treated below at least in passing, however, both as parts of a life's work and as foils for the more innovative pieces. The poems are considered under two major categories, didactic and lyric. While useful, these classes should be understood more as conveniences than as absolutes, for we shall see that the boundaries between them are often fluid. The poems are further subdivided according to certain formal and thematic criteria within each group.[2]

Didactic Poetry

Much of Claudius's poetry entails a discussion with the literature of both past and present and with the issues of the times. This discussion is conducted in two different ways. Some of the poems contain explicit literary or sociopolitical criticism or commentary on matters of a more general or occasional nature. While attesting less to Claudius's formal virtuosity than to his many interests and responses to events, they nevertheless reflect attitudes and even stylistic features typical of the work as a whole. Other poems reveal an implicit or oblique criticism of literature and the times. Claudius's approach in these pieces is especially significant, since it exhibits traits central even to the lyric poetry and the prose as well. In both types of poem the ethos is predominantly didactic, which lends credence to the contention that wide areas of the poetry—and, one might add, of the creative prose, too—are in a sense extensions of the reviews in another medium.[3]

Explicit Didacticism. Claudius's overt discussion with literature, most prominent during the 1770s, has many faces and forms. With "Alte und neue Zeit" [Past and present] he takes up the continuing quarrel between the ancients and moderns in a short, pointed madrigallike form.[4] While Minerva merited the owl in Homer's time, she now, in the age of Voltaire, "the wise and castrated man," sooner deserves the cuckoo. However, Claudius was not at all oblivious to the achievements of modern writers. In "Ich wüßte nicht warum?" [I wouldn't know why] he begins rhetorically, "Imitate Greek song?", and closes with a familiar mixture of naiveté and learning, "Videatur ["see"] cousin Ossian."[5] At the same time, he was aware of the extravagances and presumptuousness of Bardism, as we have seen.

Indeed, Claudius takes his fellow writers to task for numerous abuses. In a verse narrative called "Die Probeschrift" [A poetic attempt], for example, he allows a would-be poet to reveal his ineptness himself.[6] Then, he suggests that "Friend Franze" may sing Anacreontic songs "So viel'r will, nur ein Dichter / Freund Franze, ist Er nicht, Er" ("As much as you like, but a poet / Friend Franze, you are not, you"), an impossible rhyme, *Dichter* and *nicht, Er,* furnishing the appropriate barb.

Much of Claudius's explicit social criticism in verse is presented by two short-term but loquacious members of his fictional family, Hinz and Kunz, the German equivalents of Tom, Dick, and Harry. While departing after Book III, they make good use of their brief stay to express their opinions on several social types and conditions in pithy and pointed fashion and often in free madrigal form.[7] In one piece Hinz praises his son's many gifts—his robust rotundity, ability to spell, and knack of displaying great interest in the evening prayer, while pinching the others under the table.[8] Asked what he thinks of the youth, Kunz answers, "By my soul, there's a preacher in him!" In another, Kunz asks his friend how many doctors there are in Paris and suggests perhaps a hundred.[9] Hinz replies that there must be more, for the death list contains twenty thousand every year.

In their social origin and character Hinz and Kunz bear a strong resemblance to Fritz and the other ingenues of Claudius's work. If they demonstrate less emotion and greater pragmatism, these men from the common folk share with their fellows a certain natural, uncomplicated attitude toward life. Indeed, it is this simplicity which enables them to gain insights into the world about them. Similar to the conversations and correspondences among Asmus and *Vetter* and Andres, these discoveries emerge from the dialectic of the dialogue form. Through common-sense observation and the interplay of their perspectives Hinz and Kunz penetrate everyday reality and extract aspects of its meaning, usually in the pointed, humorous manner of the fable and verse narrative.

A goodly portion of Claudius's overtly political verse assumes the laconic, barbed form of the poems discussed heretofore. In "Eine Fabel" [A fable], which first appeared in 1795, Claudius approached a subject which was very current in the realms of philosophy and theology as well as politics.[10] Some time in the past representatives of the learned animal world petitioned the lion to relieve the bear of his duties as censor, finding it inappropriate and petty to have to haggle with him in order to publish their works. The lion, on due consideration, proclaimed freedom of the press and imprisoned the bear. His voice no sooner died down, however, than the clever rams grew silent, and scorpions, vipers, and the like began to flood the land with treatises on every subject under the sun, all different and all correct. Having reckoned on noblemindedness and love of truth, the lion shook his head and declared, " 'They weren't worth it, the bunglers, great and small; / *Let the bear loose again*!' "

The transparency of Claudius's sentiment was not lost on his fellows, for the piece earned him many enemies and numerous critiques in literary form from among those who cherished the policy of free expression introduced in Denmark in the early 1770s.[11] The question of his judgment per se, understandable considering his world-view, need not occupy us here. For our purposes, however, it is important to recognize that Claudius's contemporaries responded precisely to his judgment and not to the work as literature. This has generally been the case ever since, and not only with regard to this later work alone. Claudius's fable is no masterpiece. With its humorous digressiveness and rather witty satire, ending in an unexpected *pointe,* however, it fulfills the traditional requirements of the form and is certainly no worse than many another less controversial work. Indeed, the uproar it created is, at least to some extent, a measure of its purely literary success, such as it is. If Claudius's late work is wanting, its weakness must be sought elsewhere.

Not all of Claudius's more direct political criticism assumes the form and tone of these pieces. In "Der Schwarze in der Zuckerplantage" [The black on the sugar plantation] he imagined the experience of slaves such as those owned by Schimmelmann himself.[12] While retaining the short, free form of other political verse, he allows the downtrodden bondman to express his misery in the immediacy of the first person. His most comprehensive declaration of political principle in verse appears in the straightforward folksong form of "Kron und Szepter, 1795" [Crown and scepter, 1795], which begins with the words,

> These are no *human* belongings,
> As it's commonly said,
> They were originally gifts of *heaven,*
> *Holy* implements.[13]

Claudius's frank conversation with the times leads beyond literary and sociopolitical matters to questions of morality and religion. His reflections appear typically in the time-honored form of the proverb and are collected in part in "Ein gülden ABC" [A golden ABC] and "Ein silbern Dito" [A silver ditto].[14] Their trenchancy is reflected in the fact that they were memorized by countless schoolchildren well into the twentieth century.

This conversation finds expression, especially in the later work, in what may best be described as occasional poems. Here, births and birthdays, convivial gatherings, and weddings and deaths among family, friends, and royalty—all the stages of life of the extended human family—are commemorated and their significance stated in direct, uncomplicated fashion. In these pieces Claudius proceeds typically from the immediate event to its broader meaning in terms of death, politics, or religion. While no great achievements, these poems treat life as a unity and thereby reveal a parallel to much of the aesthetically more successful lyric poetry.

Implicit Didacticism. A considerable portion of Claudius's poetry criticizes literature without the specific object of censure ever being mentioned and at the same time makes statements on other subjects. That is to say, he utilizes various aspects of language and literary tradition in a nontraditional manner, which itself engenders a commentary on literature as well as extraliterary concerns.

The verse narrative "Wächter und Bürgermeister" [The watchman and the burgomaster], for example, tells of a nightwatchman who says *das Klock* when announcing the hour and a mayor who forces him to say *der Klock* instead.[15] Initially, the work gives the impression of humorously criticizing the abuse of authority by the powerful, as in certain of the fables. The impression is accurate. On further consideration, however, it becomes apparent that this criticism occurs by way of literary criticism, which makes the political critique possible in the first place.

The watchman violates the established gender of *Klock,* which is feminine *(die),* in a fanciful fashion so that it might rhyme with *das Horn* which he blows while performing his personal duties, thus, for a subjective, fundamentally artistic reason. The burgomaster also does violence to the language by insisting on *der,* which is equally wrong as far as convention is concerned and equally subjective; significantly, *der* rhymes with his offended sense of honor, *Ehr,* while other words related to his personal purview—*Rat* ("counselor"), *obstat,* and *Stadt* ("city")—form an additional rhyme. Yet, the burgomaster is unaware of the subjectivity of his language, indeed, of language in general, to which Claudius draws attention here. By compelling the watchman to suppress his equal right to self-expression, the burgomaster exposes himself to both literary and political criticism.

The contrast between town and country, hut and palace, had provided a motif for European literature since antiquity. Cultivated extensively in the Rococo lyric of the earlier eighteenth century, it had become outworn by Claudius's time. Typically, praise of country life is combined with a rejective gesture toward its counterpart. Claudius frequently employs the motif, notably in his *Bauernlieder,* and at times in the traditional manner. More often, however, he seeks not to disqualify town and palace, but rather to indicate the equal value of country and hut. In the "Abendlied eines Bauermanns" [A farmer's evening song], for example, the speaker praises his simple bread and milk but at the same time grants the king his patés and wine, for the sovereign, too, has much work to do, if different from his own.[16] By thwarting the expectations of the reader schooled on tradition, Claudius forces him to reconsider the established ethos of the motif in another light and gives it renewed life. Through his unobtrusive criticism of tradition he at the same time breaks a lance with a view which would deny the unity of society according to divine design.

Claudius does much the same thing vis-à-vis traditional genres. His game is all the more effective since he also handles these forms conventionally, often in the same book. He employs a choral or cantata form in several pieces, characterized by recitativos, mixed choirs, antiphonal singing, refrains, and the like. The "Weihnacht-Kantilene" [Christmas cantilena] and the "Osterlied" [Easter song], for example, celebrate the birth and resurrection of Christ, while "Krieg und Friede" [War and peace] expresses gratitude for benevolent rule.[17]

In certain of these works, however, Claudius goes beyond the grand themes traditionally associated with the form, or, put another way, does not attempt to approach their heights. The "Lied der Schulkinder zu —— an ihre kranke Wohltäterin" [Song of the schoolchildren in —— to their sick benefactress] manifests the same kind of thanks as "Krieg und Friede."[18] Yet, it does so within the closest, most intimate social circle, suggesting that this sphere and expressions of benevolence within it are in their own way as significant and as deserving of attention as the broader sociopolitical realm. While not composed in true cantata form, the "Motetto, *als der erste Zahn durch war*" [Motet, as the first tooth came through] continues in much the same vein. Beginning "Victory! Victory! / The little white tooth is here," and containing the line, "The tooth shall be called Alexander," the poem parodies the feats of conquerors by celebrating a common family event.[19]

Claudius could aim his implied criticism at broad literary currents as well. We have seen that he continued to write in the Rococo manner even while editing *Der Wandsbecker Bote* and saw fit to include a few of these and earlier pieces in volumes I and II of *Asmus*. Yet, even these poems are chaste in comparison to many of those written by contemporaries both at home and abroad. In other poems composed during this period he exploited the expectations of readers by now intimately acquainted with Rococo literature to lead them in quite another direction. The disparity between the two pieces entitled "Phidile" may serve as an example.

The first of these portrays budding romantic awareness, rather than sophisticated salacity, yet its erotic overtone is clear enough.[20] The title of the later piece, which continues, *"After Going Alone to Her Room Following the Wedding,"* would seem to suggest a consistent sequel to the earlier one.[21] Whatever anticipation it may arouse is immediately disappointed, however, for the poem begins with the lines, "Oh, God's blessing on you! / For you gave it to me." The quickened pulse which throbs throughout this work is accompanied not by sighs of passion, but rather by tears of joy shed in contemplation of sharing all the joys and sorrows of a marriage hallowed by tradition and religion. In this and other works Claudius confronts the often artificial and cold intellectualism of the Rococo with more realistic, warm human emotion. To this extent he reflects the sentimentalism of the 1770s.

Yet, Claudius did not fall victim to the often florid effusiveness of some of his contemporaries. The lack of restraint in his lyrical letters to the moon is rare in both prose and poetry. Indeed, where he sensed excessive emotionalism, he could be quick to respond, as his review of *Werther* and "Fritze" indicate. In the verse narrative "Die Geschichte von Sir Robert" [The story of Sir Robert] he is more drastic than his model, Christian Fürchtegott Gellert.[22] While the older poet's hero finally finds life without his love preferable to the tip of his sword, Claudius's Robert actually spills his brains before his Betty, whereupon she tells onrushing passersby banally, "He bashed his head in." This and other works, forming collectively a modest *Triumph der Empfindsamkeit,* plead like the "anti-Rococo" poems for greater realism in both literature and life.[23]

Lyric Poetry

In comparison with his predominantly didactic poetry, Claudius's lyric poetry deals more uniformly and far more immediately with his most essential concerns in life—earthly existence, family, death, and transcendence. It, too, contains entirely secular and more spiritual motifs but presents them in a primarily expressive manner. Thus, it reveals more lucidly and coherently than the didactic poems the nature of Claudius's attitude toward experience. The direct interpretation in some of these poems bears importantly on his sense of the place of such experience in life. The following pages seek to illuminate the way in which this attitude and sense inform a number of, in part, central lyric poems. They are divided into two types, secular poetry and religious poetry. Within each of these categories the poems are considered according to motif.

Secular Lyric Poetry. In view of Claudius's dualistic worldview and ambivalence toward all manifestations of temporal existence, the extent of his secular poetry may come as some surprise. Many of his poems on nature, family, and even death evince no spiritual dimension whatsoever. Yet, his formal handling of these themes within the secular context is, as we shall see now, identical to that in the more clearly religious poems and demonstrates the same attitude toward experience as well.

"Der Frühling. Am ersten Maimorgen"

Claudius's "Der Frühling. Am ersten Maimorgen" [Spring: on the first morning of May], written in the spring of 1774, is illuminating in this regard:

Heute will ich fröhlich fröhlich sein,
  Keine Weis und keine Sitte hören;
Will mich wälzen, und für Freude schrein,
  Und der König soll mir das nicht wehren;
Denn *er* kommt mit seiner Freuden Schar
  Heute aus der Morgenröte Hallen,
Einen Blumenkranz um Brust und Haar
  Und auf seiner Schulter Nachtigallen;
Und sein Antlitz ist ihm rot und weiß,
  Und er träuft von Tau und Duft und Segen–
Ha! mein Thyrsus sei ein Knospenreis,
  Und so tauml ich meinem Freund entgegen.[24]

(Today I will be merry, merry,
  Listen to no lengthy lectures;
I'll leap about, and shout for joy,
  And the king won't keep me from it;
For *he* is coming with his host of joys
  Today from dawn's red halls,
A flowered wreath around his breast and hair
  And on his shoulder nightingales;
And his face is red and white,
  And he drips with dew and scent and blessings–
Ha! let my thyrsus be a budding twig
  And I shall sway toward my friend in rapture.)

Despite his lyrical mood Claudius's persona betrays himself as the ingenue of the other works, especially at the beginning and end of the poem. The repetition of *fröhlich,* the excited, artless defiance of the ruler, the colloquial reflexive *ihm* in line 9, and the ecstatic *Ha!*

in line 11 all bespeak the naive manner of presentation to which Claudius's reader soon becomes accustomed.

Significantly, the persona defers indicating the source of his rapture until the fifth line and at this point introduces it through a highly characteristic and meaningful usage of personification. The figure of spring is endowed with certain features, which assume the form of visual imagery. Yet, some of the relatively few images address not only sight but other senses as well, the flowers of the wreath appealing to smell and the nightingales, implicitly, to sound. Other traits are, properly speaking, not images at all. *Duft,* if addressing the sense of smell, evokes no picture, while *Segen,* understood as *abundance,* alludes abstractly to all the remaining positive attributes of spring. It is no accident that *Segen* is followed by a dash or that the whole description of spring in these lines (7–10) is dominated by polysyndeton, manifested in fully seven repetitions of the conjunction *und*—as if the list of characteristics could continue ad infinitum. Indeed, the text clearly implies that it could. Having first given rein to his transport and then presented the reason for it, the persona finally offers a now deepened expression of his ecstasy.

There is no attempt here to encompass the entire phenomenon of spring through language in the manner of Brockes's *malende Poesie,* minutely detailed descriptions of nature. The older poet's faith in the power of language to comprehend nature and, by extension, all reality, is totally absent. Claudius's random selection from the innumerable aspects of spring in the summary form of personification represents a concession to the ultimate impotence of language to circumscribe reality. The dash and polysyndeton also signify a halt before its multiplicity. Moreover, the incompleteness and indirectness of Claudius's presentation of spring suggest identical qualities in the perception of spring. That is to say, Claudius's persona apprehends nature not as a whole, but only in part and in a general way; its fullness and essence remain hidden from him.

Brockes's belief in the capacity of rational observation to master reality, apparently self-evident to one who looks closely enough, is also missing here. Indeed, spring does not speak to the persona's reason as so many observable and reducible phenomena. Rather, it presents itself to him in the form of personal experience of the most immediate kind, human encounter, and elicits a corresponding, highly emotional response. The poem begins and ends with the persona's affective reaction to the coming of spring; spring itself appeals to his various senses. It is his sensibility which provides his access to nature, imperfect as it is, and the linguistic medium for his expression of it.[25]

In comparison with the rationalistic, descriptive and didactic poetry of Brockes and others, Claudius's treatment of nature in this poem represents a radically different perspective—and implicit criticism. His persona, still very much the ingenue, figures importantly here, for he suggests to the reader the superiority of a guileless, emotional openness to experience to a more learned approach. His artlessness, which results in a certain humor, also vitiates the sentimentality possible due to the disposition of the poem. However, Claudius does not go as far as the young Goethe and the Romantics. His persona meets spring as a friend but as an object all the same; he does not melt into oneness with it. Inasmuch as the poem focuses on the impact of spring on the experiencing subject, the object itself retains only relative importance. Vernal nature is in itself less significant than the individual human being responding to it.

"Ein Lied *hinterm Ofen zu singen*"

While nature appears as a friend in "Der Frühling" and many other works, it is far less amicable in a number of Claudius's poems.[26] A most notable example of its malevolent side is found, rather unexpectedly, in "Ein Lied *hinterm Ofen zu singen*" [A song to be sung behind the stove], first published in Book IV of the collected works:

Der Winter ist ein rechter Mann,
  Kernfest und auf die Dauer;
Sein Fleisch fühlt sich wie Eisen an,
  Und scheut nicht Süß noch Sauer.

War je ein Mann gesund, ist er's;
  Er krankt und kränkelt nimmer,
Weiß nichts von *Nachtschweiß* noch *Vapeurs,*
  Und schläft im kalten Zimmer.

Er zieht sein *Hemd* im Freien an,
  Und läßt's vorher nicht wärmen;
Und spottet über Fluß im Zahn
  Und Kolik in Gedärmen.

Aus Blumen und aus Vogelsang
  Weiß er sich nichts zu machen,

Haßt *warmen* Drang und *warmen* Klang
Und alle *warme* Sachen.

Doch wenn die Füchse bellen sehr,
Wenn's Holz im Ofen knittert,
Und um den Ofen Knecht und Herr
Die Hände reibt und zittert;

Wenn Stein und Bein vor Frost zerbricht
Und Teich' und Seen krachen;
Das klingt ihm gut, das haßt er nicht,
Denn will er sich totlachen.–

Sein Schloß von Eis liegt ganz hinaus
Beim Nordpol an dem Strande;
Doch hat er auch ein Sommerhaus
Im lieben Schweizerlande.

Da ist er denn bald dort bald hier,
Gut Regiment zu führen.
Und wenn er durchzieht, stehen wir
Und sehn ihn an und frieren.[27]

(Old Winter is a manly man,
Stout-hearted, sound, and steady;
His flesh feels just like iron and,
Come snow, come blow, he's ready.

If ever man was well, it's he;
He's never sick or sickly,
Knows naught of *night sweat* or *vapors,*
And sleeps in chilly chamber.

He puts his *shirt* on out of doors,
And doesn't have it warmed first;
And makes a mock of teeth that ache
And cholic in the bowels.

For flowers and for song of birds
He wouldn't give a nickel,
He hates *warm* longing and *warm* sound
And all things *warm.*

But when the foxes bark aloud,
  When wood in hearth is snapping,
And man and master stand close by
  And rub their hands and tremble;

When stone and bone both break with frost
  And ponds and lakes are cracking;
That sounds just fine, that he finds great,
  Then he laughs himself to death.–

Near the North Pole upon the strand
  He has an icy castle;
Likewise in lovely Switzerland
  He has a summer bower.

There up and down and all around,
  He rules his cold dominion,
And when he passes through we stand
  And look at him and shiver.)

This poem is one of Claudius's most popular, reflected by the musical settings it has inspired and by its frequent inclusion in schoolbooks and other anthologies. Its simplicity and vividness, its musicality and humor, which have led to its being viewed as a children's song, will likely assure it continued life. Yet, in and behind these features lies a view of experience identical to that examined in the previous pages.

Nowhere is it stated outright that the weather is cold. Yet, the sense of a wintry landscape exuded by the poem, much like Shakespeare's "Winter" in *Love's Labour's Lost,* is virtually palpable. This sense is owing in part to numerous optical images such as *Holz im Ofen* and the *Knecht und Herr* standing nearby, which appear throughout the poem and create far greater plasticity than in "Der Frühling." Given the nature of such imagery, however, the sound of foxes barking in the distance at once expands the cold countryside and brings it home to the shivering listener, while reference to the song of birds and warm sounds intensifies it by contrast. The coldness becomes tangible in the rubbing of hands, the pain of toothaches and cholic, and, again by contrast, the allusion to warm longing—emotion. Indeed, even the optical images address other senses: the flesh *feels* like iron, the flowers implicitly smell, and the wood in the hearth snaps.

As in "Der Frühling" as well, one notes the polysyndetic, and paratactic, connections of the various clauses, especially in strophes 1 through 4, 7, and part of 8. The sixth strophe, which ends the "description" of winter proper, is followed by the telling dash. And the abstraction of most of the random aspects of the season presented in the poem in the personification of winter is carried even further here than in the earlier poem.

All these stylistic features—the assault of the imagery and references on most of the senses and the emotions, the largely additive syntactical pattern, and the desultory subsuming of numerous characteristics of winter in the immediate and emotion-charged form of personification—all express with great success the same attitude toward language and the structure of experience as "Der Frühling." Here, more so than there, the limitations of language, the indirect, partial, and emotional nature of the encounter with reality, and the ultimate opaqueness of reality itself are clear.

Again it is thanks mainly to the humorous naiveté of the persona that the poem does not fall into the extreme, the lament, latent in it. In Claudius's work humor can leaven both negative and positive experience with sobriety. However, it cannot conceal the fact that his persona meets nature and reality as an object, and one of a particular kind.

Indeed, the distance between nature on the one hand and man and the sympathetic reader on the other is greater here than in "Der Frühling." The song is indeed to be sung behind the stove in the security of one's own four walls, for winter holds almost demonic sway over the subjugated human race. Winter is "a manly man" in a way that no man ever was. He mocks men's weaknesses and hates their pleasures; he laughs himself to death over the suffering he brings. In strophes 5 and 6 and the second half of 8, the only parts of the poem where man is mentioned directly, polysyndeton and parataxis yield to hypotaxis, which reflects syntactically the physical and emotional hold he has over men. Man can do little else than stand, watch, and shiver. If most of the poem describes winter, rather than man, in its unique way, it does so strictly in terms of the season's effect on man. This fact, combined with the two or three direct illustrations of man's response to winter, lead one to conclude again that the individual and the nature of his experience are more important than the particular object of experience.

"Der Tod"

While hostile winter replaces friendly spring, nature itself is supplanted by other objects of experience in Claudius's secular poetry. "Der Tod" [Death], which appeared in Book VI of *Asmus,* has despite, or because of, its brevity remained among his most compelling works:

> Ach, es ist so dunkel in des Todes Kammer,
> Tönt so traurig, wenn er sich bewegt
> Und nun aufhebt seinen schweren Hammer
> Und die Stunde schlägt.[28]
>
> (Oh, it is so gloomy in the chamber of death,
> Sounds so dreary, when he moves about
> And now lifts his heavy hammer up
> And strikes the hour.)

Here, one finds a vaguely contoured but objective vision of death's sphere and of Death himself as he goes about his momentous task. The predominance of open vowels in stressed syllables lends the poem a hollowness which corresponds to the nature of the vision summoned. The d's, t's, and k's give the trochaic meter a plodding quality in the first two lines. The pace quickens with the f, s, sch, and v and the h's of the third line but comes to a heavy halt with the return to plosives in the abbreviated final line. Thus, the rhythm of the poem manifests acoustically the deliberate, inexorable process of death.

In this poem the object of experience all but disappears; the cessation of life and all the images and emotions it evokes are condensed into one representative personification. There are no cries of agony or pleas for help, no expressions of hope. The only signs of empirical reality—the chamber, recalling the bedroom of the dying, and the striking of the hour, which elicits the sexton's tolling of the knell—fade from their original contexts into the controlling vision.[29] Following lines of six and five feet, the final trimeter with its pounding abruptness suggests not only the end of life but also the inadequacy of the attempt to penetrate the stark mystery of death. The obliquity and partiality of the expression of experience are greater here than perhaps in any of Claudius's other works.

The persona, too, almost disappears behind the vision. However, the very first word of the poem, *Ach,* indicates both his presence and the nature of his experience. The persona describes and narrates the brief but powerful vision from the detachment of the third person. Yet, he does so in terms of its effect on him. The chamber is *dunkel,* indeed, *so dunkel,* Death's movements sound *so traurig,* his hammer is *heavy,* and he *strikes* the hour. The visual image of Death itself is accompanied by other, highly emotionalized appeals to the senses of sight, touch, and sound; the *Ach* introduces these appeals. The dependence of the source of experience on the persona is indicated by the hypotactic connection between the description of his impressions and the narration of their origin. Death is thus refracted through the persona and becomes experiential in his emotional response to it; the relationship between subject and object is the same here as in the two nature poems.

"Ein Wiegenlied bei Mondschein zu singen"

This relationship is evident even in the most intimate expressions of parental love. "Ein Wiegenlied bei Mondschein zu singen" [A lullaby to be sung by moonlight] is, next to "Abendlied," perhaps Claudius's most beloved poem. Its numerous musical settings and appearances in anthologies are complemented by several critical studies in essay form, a distinction of which few of Claudius's individual works can boast.[30] Indeed, the piece shows Claudius at his best. Motherly love is expressed here so convincingly that the reader is likely to be unaware of (and probably does not care) how it is expressed. Repeated and more detached reading reveals that it shares the essential characteristics of all of the poet's lyric poetry:

So schlafe nun du Kleine!
   Was weinest du?
Sanft ist im Mondenscheine,
   Und süß die Ruh.

Auch kommt der Schlaf geschwinder,
   Und sonder Müh:
Der Mond freut sich der Kinder,
   Und liebet sie.

Er liebt zwar auch die Knaben,
   Doch Mädchen mehr,
Gießt freundlich schöne Gaben
   Von oben her

Auf sie aus, wenn sie saugen,
  Recht wunderbar;
Schenkt ihnen blaue Augen
  Und blondes Haar.

Alt ist er wie ein Rabe,
  Sieht manches Land;
Mein Vater hat als Knabe
  Ihn schon gekannt.

Und bald nach ihren *Wochen*
  Hat Mutter mal
Mit ihm von mir gesprochen:
  Sie saß im Tal

In einer Abendstunde,
  Den Busen bloß,
Ich lag mit offnem Munde
  In ihrem Schoß.

Sie sah mich an, für Freude
  Ein Tränchen lief,
Der Mond beschien uns beide,
  Ich lag und schlief;

Da sprach sie! "Mond, oh! scheine,
  Ich hab sie lieb,
Schein Glück für meine Kleine!"
  Ihr Auge blieb

Noch lang am Monde kleben,
  Und flehte mehr.
Der Mond fing an zu beben,
  Als hörte er.

Und denkt nun immer wieder
  An diesen Blick,
Und scheint von hoch hernieder
  Mir lauter Glück.

Er schien mir unterm Kranze
  Ins Brautgesicht,
Und bei dem Ehrentanze;
  Du warst noch nicht.[31]

(So go to sleep now little girl!
  Why are you crying?
Here in the moonlight rest
  Is soft and sweet.

And slumber comes more quickly,
  And without effort:
The moon delights in children,
  And loves them.

Of course he loves little boys,
  But little girls more so,
Pours lovely gifts so friendly
  From up above

Down on them when they're nursing,
  So wonderfully;
He gives them eyes of blue
  And flaxen hair.

He is as old as a raven,
  Sees many lands;
My father as a boy
  Already knew him.

And soon after her *childbed*
  My mother once
Spoke with him about me:
  She was sitting

One evening in the valley,
  Her bosom bare,
I lay with open mouth
  In her lap.

She looked at me, for joy
  A tear ran down,
The moon shone on us both,
  I lay and slept;

She said then! "Moon, oh! shine,
  I love her so,
Shine happiness for my little one!"
  Her eyes then clung

A long time to the moon,
  And begged for more.
The moon began to quiver,
  As if he heard.

And now thinks time and again
  About that look,
And shines pure happiness
  To me below.

He shone beneath my bridal wreath
  Into my face,
And during my wedding dance;
  You weren't there yet.)

The persona's experience is couched here in an abbreviated form of the folk song, iambic trimeters and dimeters alternating regularly in quatrains governed by regularly alternating end rhyme. Few "literary tricks" are employed. Aside from a small number of judiciously implemented figures, the forty-eight lines of the poem require nothing but literal imagery to create and narrate their few concrete, intimate scenes and events. The mother's unpretentious language and its liquid musicality, due chiefly to the predominance of alliterative fricatives and assonant open vowels, arise so naturally from the situation as to lull the reader into near total unawareness.

In the first two lines of the initial strophe the mother begins her lullaby as any mother might, telling her baby to go to sleep and asking why it is crying. The next two lines and the following strophe indicate almost imperceptibly the reason why it should not cry—the presence of the moon, referred to first simply as moonlight but then as a living agent which delights in children. From the third strophe on the moon appears in fully personified form and determines the point of view of the poem for almost the next three strophes. The psychology of the moment, with the moon apparently bathing the baby girl in its light, suggests that the moon is the source of all her beauty and implicitly, for the moment, of the mother's bliss as well. One suspects that he would favor little boys if he had found one lying in this mother's arms.

The explanation for his discernment is found in the fifth strophe, where his great age, wisdom, and experience emerge from the simile "old as a raven" and the line "sees many lands." Here, too, the point of view shifts briefly to that of the persona's father, who knew the moon even as a little boy. In the following strophe the perspective changes once again to that of her mother, which governs the poem until the next-to-last strophe. In this part of the poem the present moment and the essence of its intimate experience are expanded and portrayed in the re-creation of an identical moment in the past. Whether a recollection of talks with her mother, like the one she is now holding with her baby, or the result of imaginative projection, this reenactment reflects the identity of past and present in the persona's mind.

The ever-observant and benevolent moon, which seems to tremble with emotion through the tear-filled, retrospective eye of the persona, blesses mother and child now as it had a generation ago and through all preceding generations. It had begun to shower happiness on them even at the mother's wedding and during her wedding dance, symbol of the act of love which gave life to the baby. It was not there *yet.* But then it was, and is, and, implicitly, will become a mother like its own and like her mother and so on down through future generations. The open end of the poem is complemented by the "open" beginning, by "So," which suggests the continuation of a process begun earlier. Claudius allows past and future to converge here briefly into a three-dimensional omnipresent.

Motherly love is expressed as immediately in this poem as perhaps anywhere in literature, and yet, just as in the winter song, the motif is never stated openly. It is communicated not so much by the persona herself as by the moon and her mother along the psychological byway of something that resembles Jung's collective memory and informs experience through her. Indeed, she does not *express* her experience as much as she *narrates* it from the distance of the third person. As a result the emotion of the poem, which reaches a height in the diacope in the ninth strophe, "Mond, oh! scheine, / Ich hab sie lieb, / Schein Glück für meine Kleine!," loses much of its sentimentality.

The indirection of the persona's simple presentation of experience is accompanied once more by incompleteness of expression. Couched again in polysyndetic and paratactic syntax, open both at beginning and end, and borne by a personification and two functionally fictitious figures in a seemingly timeless instant, the experience represents a momentary glimpse of the eternal rather than a full and permanent possession. Even in its transience, however, the moment is of utmost importance, and not only in terms of this particular motif and poem. The confluence of the perspectives of past, present, and future in it prepares the way for a kind of secular epiphany. That is to say, a mother's love for her child appears here as an almost mythical power which transcends time, place, and person. Emerging together with the attitude toward the nature and structure of experience discussed earlier, such an appearance suggests the openness of this attitude and Claudius's personae to transcendence in general. We shall see that the transcendent entity need not always be secular.

The experience expressed here is intensely personal and joyful. Just as in "Der Frühling," however, Claudius's persona does not become one with it. Rather, she "meets" it from the considerable psychological distance created by the perspectivistic manner of presentation. Claudius allows his persona to project the ultimate source of her experience beyond herself through her mother to a second remove. In the tenth strophe the moon begins to quiver, "Als hörte er." Here, he reflects what is really her own experience and less its cause than its emotional effect on her. This he does in the subjunctive and in one of only two hypotactic clauses in the whole poem, indicating the dependence of its mission on her. Motherly love, as it appears here, is quite as much an object, distinct from the persona, as nature and death are in the earlier poems.

Religious Lyric Poetry. The poems in this section are discussed, for lack of a better term, under the conventional heading "religious poetry." We shall see that not all of them need necessarily be interpreted in a religious sense. However, they all further our understanding of the role of transcendence and religion in Claudius's experience and work beyond that provided by the secular lyric and didactic poetry, to which they are nonetheless in varying ways and degrees closely related. They do this largely because they, more than any others, treat the final concerns of life not only more uniformly and immediately, but comprehensively as well. Drawing two or more of these motifs into their pale at once, they each and as a group reflect the unity of Claudius's experience and expression of life.

"Der Mensch"

Claudius made one of his most general statements on earthly life in a poem entitled "Der Mensch" [Man], which appeared in Book IV of the collected works. Like Jacques's speech on the Seven Ages of Man in *As You Like It* and his own *Impetus philosophicus,* discussed in Chapter 3, the work represents a Midrash on Ecclesiastes:

Empfangen und genähret
  Vom Weibe wunderbar
Kömmt er und sieht und höret,
  Und nimmt des Trugs nicht wahr;
Gelüstet und begehret,
  Und bringt sein Tränlein dar;
Verachtet, und verehret;
  Hat Freude, und Gefahr;
Glaubt, zweifelt, wähnt und lehret,
  Hält nichts, und alles wahr;
Erbauet, und zerstöret;
  Und quält sich immerdar;
Schläft, wachet, wächst, und zehret;
  Trägt braun und graues Haar etc.
Und alles dieses währet,
  Wenn's hoch kommt, achtzig Jahr.
Denn legt er sich zu seinen Vätern nieder,
Und er kömmt nimmer wieder.[32]

(Conceived and nurtured
  By woman wondrously
He comes and sees and hears,
  And does not sense the deceit;
Covets and desires,
  And offers up his tear;
Despises, and reveres;
  Knows joy, and danger;
Believes, doubts, presumes, and teaches,
  Thinks nothing, and everything true;
Builds, and destroys;
  And is forever tormented;
Sleeps, wakes, grows, and wastes away;
  Wears hair of brown and gray, etc.
And all of this continues,
  At the outside, eighty years.
Then he lays himself down beside his fathers,
And he never returns.)

The persona of this poem presents various stages, endeavors, and experiences of human life here in additive, randomly ordered, and contrastive pairs and in clauses characterized largely by parataxis. The *etc.* at the end of line 14, forming a feminine ending in what according to the established pattern should be a masculine line, has the effect of an afterthought and enhances the self-evident nature of this desultory, contradictory order. These devices reflect the multiplicity of life and the inability of language and the experience borne by it to comprehend life in its totality. Indeed, the repetition of the clauses in independent lines, the steady iambic-trimeter rhythm, and the two rhymes which control the poem almost to its end create a formal regularity which suggests by contrast that disorder and contradiction themselves are the order of life. The retarding pentameter and return to the original meter at the end of the poem, complemented by a change in rhyme, support formally the concluding statement on the senselessness of earthly existence.

As in "Der Tod," the persona almost vanishes as a mediating force behind an apparently objective description of human life. The formal regularity mentioned above, the sonorous vowels, and the sibilants f and v, which recur fully twenty times, lend the presentation a detached, matter-of-fact quality. However, his attitude toward his subject emerges, if indirectly, at the very beginning of the work.

The first four lines both anticipate and comment on what follows in the piece. Man bears the security and certainty of the home (ll. 1–2) with him in his general approach to life (l. 3), the latter modified grammatically and colored emotionally by the former. Because of his expectations he does not perceive the illusoriness of his varied experience (l. 4). Far from being an aside, as has been contended, this line is pivotal.[33] For it, too, is modified by line 1 and, standing, as it were, in apposition to line 3, interprets them both from a position of superior knowledge. Since it ends with a semicolon, moreover, the pairs of contradictions which follow function as so many illustrations of the statement and comment in lines 1 through 4. The new sentences contained in the final four lines both continue the preceding description and provide an implicit, now deepened justification of line 4.

The deception mentioned there lies, accordingly, in man's failure to recognize the senselessness of his passionate, contradictory immersion in a life subject to physical death. Viewed with an eye to its ultimate goal, as it is in this poem, earthly existence appears devoid of meaning. The persona himself does not fall victim to this delusion, however, for he is able to step back from life and to portray and evaluate it from the sovereign remove of the third person. His involvement is real but at the same time distanced and dispassionate.

One can understand the attitude toward life expressed in this poem secularly as the sum of one individual's experience of earthly life. Like *Impetus philosophicus,* the poem lacks the overt transcendental dimension which in Ecclesiastes shelters human existence like a sacred canopy. So understood, the work is as pessimistic a judgment of the human condition as one is likely to find in the optimistic eighteenth century. However, the allusion to Ecclesiastes and the clear reference to Psalms 90:10 in lines 15 and 16 suggest the recourse offered by the Old Testament. And the superior perspective of the persona may be seen as deriving not from earthly experience alone but from the divine inspiration of the Old Testament writer as well. The attitude toward existence *can* be understood in the theological sense of *vanitas mundi,* whereby the true meaning of life—a concept not limited to the phenomenal world—lies in the realm of transcendence. The persona's inner distance to life and his peaceful tone, which differ markedly from Baroque treatments of the theme, speak for such an interpretation and for a literal acceptance of the implications of the complex.

The secular mood of the poem is quite strong, however, and a theological interpretation is but one—and the less immediate—of two possibilities. Even accepting the inspiration of transcendence, the evaluation of earthly life remains extremely dark. Yet, the possibility does exist. One may view the experience of life expressed in the piece as positing indirectly the existence of a transcendental reality, here, in contrast to the poem on motherly love, of a specifically religious nature.

"Täglich zu singen"

Claudius published "Täglich zu singen" [To be sung daily], one of his most beloved and often musically adapted poems, in the *Adreß-Comptoir-Nachrichten* in 1777 and included it in Book III of *Asmus* the following year. The work, a daily song of thanks and praise, contains a general statement on life, as does "Der Mensch," but how different its mood:

> Ich danke Gott, und freue mich
> Wie's Kind zur Weihnachtsgabe,
> Daß ich bin, bin! Und daß ich dich,
> Schön menschlich Antlitz! habe;

Daß ich die Sonne, Berg und Meer,
   Und Laub und Gras kann sehen,
Und abends unterm Sternenheer
   Und lieben Monde gehen;

Und daß mir denn zumute ist,
   Als wenn wir Kinder kamen,
Und sahen, was der heil'ge Christ
   Bescheret hatte, amen!

Ich danke Gott mit Saitenspiel,
   Daß ich kein König worden;
Ich wär geschmeichelt worden viel,
   Und wär vielleicht verdorben.

Auch bet ich ihn von Herzen an,
   Daß ich auf dieser Erde
Nicht bin ein großer reicher Mann,
   Und auch wohl keiner werde.

Denn Ehr und Reichtum treibt und bläht,
   Hat mancherlei Gefahren,
Und vielen hat's das Herz verdreht,
   Die weiland wacker waren.

Und all das Geld und all das Gut
   Gewährt zwar viele Sachen;
Gesundheit, Schlaf und guten Mut
   Kann's aber doch nicht machen.

Und die sind doch, bei Ja und Nein!
   Ein rechter Lohn und Segen!
Drum will ich mich nicht groß kastein
   Des vielen Geldes wegen.

Gott gebe mir nur jeden Tag,
   Soviel ich darf zum Leben.
Er gibt's dem Sperling auf dem Dach;
   Wie sollt er's mir nicht geben![34]

(I thank God, and am as glad
   As a child with a Christmas present,
That I am, am! And that I have you,
   Fair human countenance!

That I can see the sun and mountains,
  And the sea and leaves and grass,
And walk at evening beneath the host of stars
  And the dear moon;

And that I have the feeling then,
  As when we children came,
And saw what the holy Christ child
  Had given us, amen!

I thank God with songs of harps,
  That I became no king;
I would have been much flattered then
  And maybe ruined too.

I also worship him from my heart,
  That I on this earth
Am not a great and wealthy man,
  And likely won't become one.

For wealth and honor drive and bloat,
  And bear all kinds of danger,
And have turned the hearts of many men,
  Who formerly were upright.

And all the money and all the things
  Afford a lot it's true;
But health, and sleep, and a cheerful heart
  They still cannot provide.

And yet these things are, upon my soul!
  A real reward and blessing!
So I won't make too much ado
  About a lot of money.

May God give to me every day
  Just what I need to live.
He gives it to the sparrow on the roof;
  Why shouldn't he give it to me!)

Claudius's ingenue is nowhere more in evidence than in this poem. The folk-song form, the ecstatic repetition of *bin* and the description of the moon as *lieb,* the naive "Und wohl auch keiner werde" and colloquial "bei Ja und Nein," all identify him as the simple speaker of other poems and the prose. Twice in the first strophes he expresses his experience as that of a child. In over half of the poem he explains it through the hut-palace motif and in the final strophe makes a direct wish for a simple life. Indeed, simplicity as a positive state of mind and being is thematicized in the poem.

The ingenue's expression of experience in the first three strophes is as direct, immediate, and, in contrast to "Der Mensch," as joyous as in any of Claudius's works. It is presented here and throughout most of the poem in the first person. The repetition of *bin,* all the stronger for its appearance first in an unstressed and then in a stressed syllable, suggests a oneness of persona and experience. Indeed, his state of emotion is intense enough so that the gifts for which he expresses thanks and joy are somewhat overshadowed by it. They proceed in dependent *daß*-clauses and random order from the emotion revealed in the first half of the initial strophe and end with the emotion evinced in the third.

Yet, even in these first strophes a certain detachment is noticeable. The attitude of thanks itself presupposes at least a degree of distance between the individual and experience. Moreover, the persona expresses his gratitude indirectly in the simile in strophe 1, line 2, and in the reminiscence in the third strophe. And his distance increases drastically with the introduction of the hut-palace motif, which governs strophes 4 through 8, more than half of the poem. During this long glance at the sociopolitical world the poem assumes something of the spirit of the didactic poetry. The request for the essentials of life in the final strophe is followed by a rather didactic demonstration based on an analogy to nature.

The mood of this poem, like that of "Der Mensch," is quite secular, if of an entirely different color. The reasons for thanks and joy—the human form, the landscape, the nocturnal sky—all derive from natural experience. The religious echoes which resound in the references to Christmas gifts and the sparrow can themselves be understood as originating in purely earthly experience. As the final strophe clearly indicates, however, the goodness of life is expressed by way of nature ultimately in analogy to the goodness of the creator, in which man, too, may share. And the various gifts of earthly life, enumerated haphazardly in strophes 1 and 2, are embraced by and likened to earthly symbols of the creator's gift of eternal life to man through Christ.

The concept of life—of reality—emerging from the perspectives revealed in the poem, then, extends by implication beyond the world of phenomena to the realm of transcendence. The experience of earthly joy reflects that of the spiritual world. Claudius's emotional but distanced manner of expression suggests, more strongly than in "Der Mensch," that his indirect and partial mode of experience is open to the influence of transcendence of a theological kind. While it does not enter and inform the world as substance, transcendence is nonetheless remotely and imperfectly experiential in earthly life.

The conceptual and stylistic significance of the interplay of perspectives provided by persona, nature, motif, and symbol in the expression of this reality is perhaps more apparent here than in "Der Mensch." Perspectivism is particularly important in the religious poems, especially with regard to the issue of transcendence, as we shall see over and again. The poem also demonstrates an almost casual transition from the expression of such experience to the teaching of it. The edifying purpose, only faintly perceptible in "Der Mensch," suggests here more clearly the possibility of a relationship between two literary modes usually considered inimical to each other.

"Der Tod und das Mädchen"

"Der Tod und das Mädchen" [Death and the maiden], even more so than "Der Tod," has come to represent Claudius's general attitude toward death. First published in the *Göttinger Musenalmanach* in 1775, it was included in the very first volume of the collected works:

Das Mädchen
Vorüber! Ach, vorüber!
Geh wilder Knochenmann!
Ich bin noch jung, geh Lieber!
Und rühre mich nicht an.

Der Tod
Gib deine Hand, du schön und zart Gebild!
Bin Freund, und komme nicht, zu strafen.
Sei gutes Muts! ich bin nicht wild,
Sollst sanft in meinen Armen schlafen![35]

(*The Maiden*
Go past me! Oh, go past me!
Go wild skeleton!

I am still young, go dear one!
And do not touch me.

Death
Give me your hand, you fair and tender shape!
I'm a friend, and haven't come to punish.
Be of good cheer! I am not wild,
You shall sleep softly in my arms!)

Here, much as in "Der Tod," death and all of its associations are compressed into Claudius's unique variation of the Grim Reaper motif. The experiencing persona of most other works itself emerges from the relative anonymity of "Der Tod" and the poems previously discussed as an acting figure. The two confront each other in the immediacy of a dialogue strongly reminiscent of the medieval disputation and dance of death. Despite the new configuration the object exists here, as earlier, for the sake of the subject and its influence on her.

The maiden's terror before the appearance of Death is reflected in the short, trimeter lines of her portion of the dialogue and especially in the staccato rhythm of the first line. The caesuras after each syllable of the second foot here break the line into three metrically fragmented parts, producing an inarticulateness corresponding to her fear. Only in the second line is she able to formulate her plea for mercy coherently. The caesura following the second foot of the third line has a similar but less intense effect, while the fourth line, which lacks the caesuras and exclamation mark of the earlier lines, indicates an even greater abatement of emotion. The preponderance of closed and short vowels lends an appropriate shrillness to her cry.

The maiden uses all the means at her disposal to move Death. She in a sense insults him by calling him *wild* and alluding to his ugliness, refers to her youth in an appeal to his compassion, and goes so far as to flatter him by addressing him as *Lieber*. It has been suggested that this appellation alludes to the rejection of the suing lover by the coy maiden.[36] This contention would seem to be supported by the noticeably diminished emotion in the third and fourth lines as well as by the nature and manner of Death's response to her entreaty.

Death's reply to the maiden is cast in lengthier lines, a pentameter and three tetrameters, and exhibits a much smoother rhythm. Its characteristic long, open vowels create a sonority foreign to the maiden's imploration. These formal features accord with his omnipotence and conciliatory approach to the terrified girl. He woos her, asking for her hand, and, in his turn, flatters her by referring to her beauty and tenderness. Indeed, he seeks to draw her into his embrace figuratively as well as literally by embedding her cries in his own, broader statements. The trimeter arising after the comma in his first line answers formally and semantically to her second line; she adverts to his ugliness, and he alludes magnanimously to her loveliness. The trimeter following *Freund* in his second line, where he says he has not come to punish her, attempts to allay the fear expressed throughout her three-stressed lines.[37] And the phrase "ich bin nicht wild" in his third line forms another semantic response to the accusation in her second line.

The two strophes are also connected by end rhyme and line endings. The ü-a-ie-a scheme of the maiden's strophe is repeated and varied in the i-a-i-a pattern of Death's, the variation lying in the greater openness of the vowels in the second stanza. While weak, feminine endings govern the one, strong, masculine endings control the other. This is true even of the superscriptions, *Das Mädchen* and *Der Tod.* Down to the smallest units of sound and meter Death tries to surround and absorb the fearful maiden, this most vibrant species of human life. As lover or as friend, *Freund Hain* seeks to bring the human soul to eternal rest and peace.

His desire is not fulfilled, however, for the poem ends before the moment of death itself occurs. Here, Claudius once again yields to the mystery of the experience, as he had done throughout the poem. As in the earlier pieces, personification remains an immediate but abstract, indirect means of presenting the source of experience. Expressed as a visionary encounter with this abstraction, the experience itself in the figure of the maiden shares this obliquity and incompletion. At the same time the object of experience has meaning only in terms of the emotionally experiencing subject. The form of Death's strophe and the will manifested in it are conditioned by and relative to their counterparts in the maiden's stanza.

But just what is the nature of Death's impact on the maiden? The human and natural element of the experience, the terror before impending annihilation, has rightfully been stressed.[38] At the same time it has been emphasized to the exclusion of a Christian interpretation of the experience as the transition to eternal life. Now, the girl's response to Death's mollifying words lies beyond the poem; her fear and his consolation remain *formally* balanced within the dialogue. However, the poem reveals a *contextual* movement toward the possibility of greater knowledge and a corresponding change in her position. Death has the final word, which indicates that the maiden's fear is, if natural and understandable, ultimately groundless. For he is not wild; quite the contrary, *she* is. Yet, she shows signs of yielding to him even before he speaks. The ending of the poem, which is far more positive than that of "Der Tod," leaves open the possibility that she—and the reader—will draw appropriate conclusions for their own lives. This movement and the potential for change of position lend the poem something of the didactic character mentioned earlier.

The conclusions reached by the reader need not necessarily be of a Christian nature. The secular character of the poem is again pronounced. However, one cannot fail to hear Luther's biblical German behind Death's phrase "Sei gutes Muts!", which recurs almost verbatim or as "Sei [d] getrost" ("Be of good cheer") or in the reverse, "Fürchte [t] dich [euch] nicht" ("Fear not"), throughout the New Testament, where fear of death and the possibility of salvation are expressed. "Sei gutes Muts" is indeed the fundamental exhortation of Christianity. In this poem, just as in the others discussed, Claudius reveals an attitude toward experience which admits of religious transcendence.

"Christiane"

If "Der Tod und das Mädchen" treats the theme of death in general terms, a number of other poems present it in a more specific context. Claudius wrote at least three on the deaths of his children, two for Christiane and one for his second son named Matthias.[39] While stemming initially from one area of experience, these three pieces unite motifs and important features of other religious poems, indeed, of Claudius's works as a whole, and reveal the full breadth of his experience of life and death and his poetic representation of reality.

"Christiane," the first of these poems to be considered here, appeared originally in Book VI of *Asmus:*

Es stand ein Sternlein am Himmel,
Ein Sternlein guter Art;

Das tät so lieblich scheinen,
So lieblich und so zart!

Ich wußte seine Stelle
Am Himmel, wo es stand;
Trat abends vor die Schwelle,
Und suchte, bis ich's fand;

Und blieb denn lange stehen,
Hatt große Freud in mir:
Das Sternlein anzusehen;
Und dankte Gott dafür.

Das Sternlein ist verschwunden;
Ich suche hin und her
Wo ich es sonst gefunden,
Und find es nun nicht mehr.[40]

(A little star stood in the heavens,
A little star of good sort;
It shone so sweetly,
So sweetly and softly!

I knew its place
In the heavens, where it stood;
Went evenings before the threshold,
And looked until I found it;

And then stood a long time
And was filled with great joy:
To look upon the little star;
And thanked God for it.

The little star has vanished;
I look now here now there
Where I was wont to find it,
And find it now no more.)

Here Claudius presents what, without the title and our knowledge of the biographical background, could be taken as an expression of an experience of nature. In the first of these abbreviated folk-song strophes he uses the simplest, almost banal language to evoke the beauty of the star—two brief, descriptive statements (ll. 1 and 3) with a hint of personification *(gut, lieblich, zart)*. The last strophe affirms the disappearance of the star and the persona's vain attempts to find it. Read with a view to the title and source of inspiration, however, personified nature becomes an extended metaphor of a human being; the beauty and vanishing of a star prove to be a silent expression in analogy to nature of the ultimately inexpressible beauty and death of a loved one.

Significantly, less attention is devoted to the star or daughter, the ostensible subject of the poem, than to the persona. The star has, as it were, an independent identity only in the initial lines of the first and final strophes. In all other parts of the poem it exists only through the persona's experience of it. Despite the immediacy of the experience, its expression is oblique. The persona's intimate involvement manifests itself less as an emotional inner state than as reflection and action: He *knew* its location, *went* before the door, *looked* until he *found* it, *stood* for a long time *watching* it, etc. Only in the second line of the third strophe does he speak of his joy outright. The literal and metaphysical remove of the star and the objective, matter-of-fact manner of presentation create an enormous psychological distance between the persona and the source of his experience. As in so many other lyric poems, the central figure of the piece experiences reality as an engaging but remote object.

Just as in "Der Tod und das Mädchen" and other of Claudius's works, the experience presented here can be interpreted in purely secular terms. The perspectives created by the persona and the motifs of death and nature may be viewed as stemming from natural phenomena illuminating each other mutually within an earthly frame of reference. However, the star has had a varied symbolic life in Christian tradition, not of least importance as a representation of the human soul. Its disappearance in this poem—and with it the spirit of Christiane—can be seen in a religious sense as a returning home to the transcendental realm of eternity. The real and figurative distance of the star from earth and its proximity to the "heavens" as well as the persona's physical and psychological detachment make such a view all the more plausible. Yet, the possibility of transcendence exists only as symbol, and the relationship of the poem to it remains at best ambivalent.

"Bei ihrem Grabe"

The perspectives which inform "Christiane" reveal a quite different configuration in "Bei ihrem Grabe" [At her grave], the second of these poems, which first appeared in *Jacobis Überflüssiges Taschenbuch* in 1800:

Diese Leiche hüte Gott!
 Wir vertrauen sie der Erde,
Daβ sie hier von aller Not
 Ruh, und wieder Erde werde.

Da Liegt sie, die Augen zu
 Unterm Kranz, im Sterbekleide! . . .
Lieg und Schlaf in Frieden du;
 Unsre Lieb und unsre Freude!

Gras und Blumen gehn herfür,
 Alle Samenkörner treiben,
Treiben–und sie wird auch hier
 In der Gruft nicht immer bleiben.

Ausgesät nur, ausgesät
 Wurden alle die, die starben;
Wind- und Regenzeit vergeht,
 Und es kommt ein Tag der Garben.

Alle Mängel abgetan
 Wird sie denn in bessern Kränzen
Still einhergehn, und fortan
 Unverweslich sein und glänzen.[41]

(May God watch over this body!
 We entrust it to the earth,
That it might rest here from all need,
 And turn to earth again.

There she lies, her eyes closed
 Beneath her wreath, in her shroud! . . .
Lie and sleep in peace;
 Our love and our joy!

Grass and flowers issue forth,
 Every grain of seed sprouts up,

Sprouts up—and she too will not always
   Stay here in the grave.

Seeded down, just seeded down
   Were all those who died;
Time of wind and rain goes by,
   And there comes a day of harvest.

Every blemish taken off
   She'll then walk softly along
In better wreaths, and from that time
   Be imperishable and shine.)

As in "Christiane," the source of experience itself, a departed, beloved daughter, occupies in its own right a minimal portion of the poem, appearing only in lines 1 and 2 of the second strophe. The first strophe expresses the wish of the personae for their daughter, the verb *vertrauen* indicating as much their attitude toward burial as the action itself. Indeed, their point of view prevails throughout most of the poem; the relationship between experiencing subjects and experienced object is the same here as in the preceding piece. The nature of their experience is expressed in part indirectly. The parataxis of the first two lines of the second strophe and the dots following them imply, as so often before, the inability of experience and language to capture fully deeply moving reality. At this point they can merely wish their daughter peace in a touching, personal address, their emotion only suggested by the exclamation marks.

In the first half of the third strophe a biblical analogy to burgeoning nature interprets the experience religiously in terms of resurrection, more directly than in "Christiane," but still from the stylistic and psychological distance of metaphor. But then something new occurs. In the second half of the strophe the personae suddenly shift from interpretation by analogy to an overt interpretation of their experience in a transcendental sense without recourse to any stylistic intermediary. The dash following *treiben* in the third line, in a manner of speaking, ironically belies itself and the ellipses in the second strophe. Standing after the analogy and followed by *und* and the direct interpretation, it indicates with the force of a semicolon the causal relationship between the two and the easy transition from the one to the other. Moreover, the emphasis placed on the active term of the analogy, *treiben,* which appears at the end and the beginning of successive lines (anadiplosis), and the three-fold rhyme formed by it and the active term of the direct interpretation, *bleiben,* lend the force of persuasion and sound to this relationship. If earthly experience and language cannot capture reality fully, Claudius's perspectivism suggests, they can nevertheless create inner certainty regarding the nature of reality, both temporal and transcendental.

It is important to note the relative value of the analogy and the state of certainty of the personae expressed in the poem. The analogy to nature initially leads the personae to conviction. This once won, however, the function of the analogy changes and becomes of secondary importance. Following the direct interpretation at the end of the third strophe, the analogy in the fourth serves not to impart new knowledge, but rather to exemplify knowledge already possessed. The personae show their mastery of nature here through their demonstration and in the fifth strophe by dropping the analogy altogether in an open declaration of faith in the eventual resurrection of their daughter. They overcome not only the immediate source of experience, understanding it within the context of total reality, but ultimately the means of their understanding as well. What remains at the end of the poem, in stark contrast to "Christiane," is their certain awareness of transcendence.

The significance of the relationship between indirect and direct methods of interpretation, as presented here, goes beyond the question of transcendence. For the transition between analogy and assertion is also one from expressivism to didacticism. If the first half of the poem evinces the experience of the personae, the second half draws conclusions from it which are applicable to the reader as well as to the personae. The second half of the third strophe is deduced from the first, and the fourth and fifth strophes represent a demonstration and a deepened restatement of its validity, respectively. Just as do "Täglich zu singen" and "Der Tod und das Mädchen," the poem reveals the compatibility of the two literary modes within Claudius's poetic world.

"Die Mutter am Grabe" and "Der Vater"

Claudius wrote "Die Mutter am Grabe" [The mother at the grave] and "Der Vater" [The father] as one piece on the death of his son Matthias and published it in Book V of *Asmus.* The two other poems written on the passing of a child reflect divergent stylistic and attitudinal approaches to transcendence. This work, in turn, departs from them both:

Die Mutter am Grabe
Wenn man ihn auf immer hier begrübe,
  Und es wäre nun um ihn geschehn;
Wenn er ewig in dem Grabe bliebe,
  Und ich sollte ihn nicht wiedersehn,
  Müßte ohne Hoffnung von dem Grabe gehn - - -
Unser Vater, o du Gott der Liebe!
Laß ihn wieder auferstehn.

Der Vater
Er ist nicht auf immer hier begraben,
  Es ist nicht um ihn geschehn!
Armes Heimchen, du darfst Hoffnung haben,
  Wirst gewiß ihn wiedersehn,
  Und kannst fröhlich von dem Grabe gehn.
Denn die Gabe aller Gaben
Stirbt nicht, und muß auferstehn.[42]

(The Mother at the Grave
If he were being buried here forever,
  And it were all over with him;
If he remained eternally in the grave,
  And I should not see him again,
  I had to leave the grave without hope - - -
Our father, oh thou God of love!
Let him rise again.

The Father
He is not buried here forever,
  It is not all over with him!
Poor little cricket, you may have hope,
  Will certainly see him again,
  And can go joyfully from the grave.
For the gift of all gifts
Does not die, and must rise again.)

Here no star, no body beneath a wreath, objectifies and distances the source of experience from the experiencing subjects, as was the case in the poems for Christiane. The death of a beloved son exists wholly and exclusively in the emotional experience of the mother and father vis-à-vis the naked fact of his demise. And their expression of this experience is as immediate as the experience itself.

The responses of the mother and father to their son's death, separated into two strophes, form a dialogue similar in some respects to that in "Der Tod und das Mädchen." Each represents a position diametrically opposed to the other, and there is a movement toward greater insight between them. In the earlier poem, however, the natural terror of the creature before impending death and its sense or senselessness were thematicized, a transcendental dimension remaining only implicit. Here, transcendence itself, in the form of resurrection after the fact of death, occupies the thematic center of the work.

The mother's doubt manifests itself in a series of five if-clauses in the subjunctive, which creates a tension both syntactic and psychological.[43] Unable or unwilling to yield to the despair inferred by her chain of thought, she pauses and then expresses a helpless plea to God, leaving the tension unresolved. However, the father counters her doubts one by one in the affirmative indicative, thus resolving the tension and moving the discussion forward to a new, greater awareness. Where the mother utters a cry for eternal life for her son, the father states its absolute certainty.

The parallelism of the two strophes, even greater than in "Der Tod und das Mädchen," thus has the same function as in that poem, but how different its thrust. The certainty of physical death is replaced here with the certainty of life after death, which the mother and the reader as well may share. And, in contrast to "Christiane" and "Bei ihrem Grabe," the expression of experience follows not in analogy to nature or any earthly perspective. The *denn,* which introduces the father's final statement of assurance, amplifies no prior temporal evidence of resurrection, but rather other personal statements of certitude. Such expressions spring from an experience of reality which goes beyond the pale of earthly existence. The "Gabe aller Gaben," which can be understood as the son of these parents, the son of God, and ultimately the human soul, refers to life in the broadest Christian sense of the word and rests as a firm possession in the father's consciousness. Claudius's experience of life is not only open to a transcendent aspect of reality, but is, at least at times, filled by it. As the structure of the work indicates, such fullness of experience admits of edification as well as of expression.

"Abendlied"

The three poems on the deaths of his children reveal the breadth of Claudius's experience and expression of transcendence, ranging from faint intimations to complete lucidity. It is important to remember that they were all first published between his fiftieth and sixtieth years, at a time when he was supposedly becoming more specifically and narrowly Christian. While the clarity of "Die Mutter am Grabe" and "Der Vater" would seem to support such a view, the varying indirection of "Bei ihrem Grabe" and "Christiane," which were written even later, tends to belie it. Other, in this respect similar late works, for example "Die Sternseherin Lise" [The star gazer Lisa], could be added to these. By the same token, the experience and expression of transcendence in these poems are not limited to the late work. Claudius's "An —— als ihm die —— starb," composed perhaps as early as 1766, reveals the continuity of his lyric poetry in this regard. Indeed, the moments of clear-sightedness represented in the poems on his son's death and a few others are, while they do occur, not characteristic of his lyric. And the experience of life predominant there is nowhere more compellingly manifested than in "Abendlied."

Herder early recognized the poem's masterful renewal of folk and hymnic traditions and included it in his collection of folk songs in 1779. It has attracted more composers than any of Claudius's other poems and, in the melody of J. A. P. Schulz, published in 1790, has gained the status of a folk song. Still appearing in schoolbooks and anthologies and discussed in general and specialized studies, it has become Claudius's most beloved and enduring work. While written around 1779, it is indeed his most characteristic work as well, if not for the reasons generally assumed:

Der Mond ist aufgegangen
Die goldnen Sternlein prangen
   Am Himmel hell und klar;
Der Wald steht schwarz und schweiget,
Und aus den Wiesen steiget
   Der weiße Nebel wunderbar.

Wie ist die Welt so stille,
Und in der Dämmrung Hülle
   So traulich und so hold!
Als eine stille Kammer,

Wo ihr des Tages Jammer
  Verschlafen und vergessen sollt.

Seht ihr den Mond dort stehen?—
Er ist nur halb zu sehen,
  Und ist doch rund und schön!
So sind wohl manche Sachen,
Die wir getrost belachen,
  Weil unsre Augen sie nicht sehn.

Wir stolze Menschenkinder
Sind eitel arme Sünder,
  Und wissen gar nicht viel;
Wir spinnen Luftgespinste,
Und suchen viele Künste,
  Und kommen weiter von dem Ziel.

Gott, laβ uns *dein* Heil schauen,
Auf nichts Vergänglichs trauen,
  Nicht Eitelkeit uns freun!
Laβ uns einfältig werden,
Und vor dir hier auf Erden
  Wie Kinder fromm und fröhlich sein!

Wollst endlich sonder Grämen
Aus dieser Welt uns nehmen
  Durch einen sanften Tod!
Und, wenn du uns genommen,
Laβ uns in Himmel kommen,
  Du unser Herr und unser Gott!

So legt euch denn, ihr Brüder,
In Gottes Namen nieder;
  Kalt ist der Abendhauch.
Verschon uns, Gott! mit Strafen,
Und laβ uns ruhig schlafen!
  Und unsern kranken Nachbar auch![44]

(The moon has risen
The golden stars are shining
  In the heavens brightly and clearly;
The forest stands dark and silent,
And from the meadows rises
  The white mist wondrously.

How calm the world is,
And in the veil of dusk
  So homey and so lovely!
Like a quiet chamber,
Where you shall sleep away and forget
  The misery of the day.

You see the moon standing there?—
Only half can be seen,
  And yet it's round and beautiful!
So are many things,
Which we deride confidently,
  Because our eyes cannot see them.

We proud creatures
Are vain, pitiful sinners,
  And know not much at all;
We spin our webs of air,
And seek many inventions,
  And come farther from the goal.

God, let us see *thy* salvation,
Trust in nothing transient,
  Rejoice not in vanity!
Let us become simple,
And before you here on earth
  Be pious and joyful like children!

Finally, without grief, please
Take us from this world
  Through a peaceful death!
And, when you've taken us,
Let us go to heaven,
  Our Lord and our God!

Now lay you down, my brothers,
To sleep in God's name;
  The evening breeze is cold.
Spare us, God! with punishment,
And let us sleep peacefully!
  And our sick neighbor, too!)

In the first strophe the persona evokes a serene nocturnal sky and landscape, described objectively but in only a few, additive impressions, far from the *malende Poesie* of Brockes. In the next he proceeds immediately from the description of nature to the emotional effect of its tranquillity on him. This is reflected not least of all by the complete prosodic regularity of the poem. Each strophe falls into two tercets, each forming a cadence indicated by appropriate punctuation. These, in turn, consist of two iambic trimeters with weak endings followed by a line with a strong ending, which resolves each cadence. The final line, a longer tetrameter, brings each strophe to rest as well and sets it apart from the next. While the cadences and strophes are thus rhythmically autonomous, they are united by the rhyme of the final line of each pair of tercets and by the *a a b c c b* rhyme scheme of each strophe. Perhaps still more revealing is the tonality of the poem. Created by largely open vowels and incessant alliteration and consonance of fricatives (v, f), sibilants (s, z, sh), and liquids (n, m), which together occur over 250 times, it is sonorous and fluid, as befits the experience of quiescence expressed.

In the second strophe as well the persona intimates the nature and significance of the emotional impact of the scene on him. It gives him a sense of the security and benevolence provided by the intimately familiar, expressed by *traulich, hold,* and the simile of a quiet bedroom. The figurative juxtaposition of nocturnal nature and the safety of sleep in one's own home suggests not only rest from the misery of the day, but, as in the dedication in Books I and II, from that of life as well. Nature represents here a more permanent home and respite. Following the pattern of most of his lyric poems, Claudius presents an emotional experience of life with its intimations of immortality from a distance both stylistic and psychological.

Yet, even here the persona forsakes total impersonality to address his readers openly (l. 5) and in the third strophe turns to them immediately. He now employs the analogy to nature as an exemplum and interprets it directly to demonstrate the reality of the unseen and the error of those who in their complacency fail to recognize it, including himself, significantly, among them. In the next strophe he expands on the conclusions of the foregoing demonstration and places them in a specifically religious context with the almost verbatim quotation from Ecclesiastes 7:29f., in line 5. While his procedure here is rationalistic, however, the analogy on which it is based is itself indirect, and his expression of the experience of transcendence remains oblique.

The evocation of God in the fifth strophe and the subsequent prayer for certainty, a meaningful and therefore simple earthly life, a peaceful death, and salvation—both stem from insights presented expressively and didactically earlier in the poem. The persona senses the reality of God and his promise deep within him and sees reflections of it in his temporal experience. At the same time he is aware that such experience provides mere reflections and considerable interference and uncertainty as well. Conscious of the gulf separating him from transcendence, he turns helplessly to God in prayer.

This separation is emphasized in the final strophe by the persona's return to his fellow men and the original nocturnal scene, where the night is now chill, no longer evoking the warmth of the figure in the second strophe. He suggests that they go to sleep in God's name, in accordance with the recognition which was gained earlier and culminated in the prayer. He then repeats his prayer for a peaceful life and sleep, implicitly both on earth and in the hereafter, and extends it to his sick neighbor, who, like himself and all men, lives in essential isolation from God.

The oblique expression of experience at the beginning of the poem, filtered through the emotionally responding persona, implies here as elsewhere the indirectness of experienced reality itself in Claudius's life and work, the inability of man and his verbal medium to encompass it completely, and the inner and, in this poem, literal distance between the experiencing subject and the source of his experience. Since transcendence itself is thematicized here, however, it also suggests, perhaps more cogently than in any other work, the openness of Claudius's experience and his ideal of simplicity of soul to a reality which goes beyond temporal existence. The change to a more didactic mood from the third strophe on indicates once more the proximity of expressivity and didacticism with Claudius. His "Abendlied" is a major expression of religious experience, all commentators have agreed. However, it represents no union of man and God through nature, unless one means by that description a union through faith.

Claudius as a Religious Writer

Earlier in this study we encountered the contention that Claudius changed from liberal involvement in mundane affairs and indirection in art during his youth to consistent and narrow Christianity and didacticism in later life, a parallel drawn between attitude and artistic expression. We saw, on the other hand, that he has also been called an atheist in the decisive moments of his life. The religious interpretation, whether viewed positively or negatively, has proven to be more lasting. We ourselves have observed a general tendency of this nature. However, we have also seen that the change is highly differentiated; it is not identical to a basic change of attitude toward the central issues of life. At this point we may summarize and further comment on the significance of our observations in the entire work, especially as they pertain to religion.

Claudius laid his pen aside from a large number of his works in both prose and poetry without interpreting them, from *Impetus philosophicus* on to "Christiane." In many others, from some of the prose satires and literary criticism in verse to the late letters to Andres, he interprets his subjects in various ways directly. Works such as "Über das Genie" and "Die Mutter am Grabe" and "Der Vater" represent mixtures of the two approaches. Thus, the salient question is less the frequency of each approach at any given time than the function of each, regardless of time or even specific theme and treatment.

Claudius's uninterpreted works are, as we have seen, characterized by a refusal to comment straightforwardly on life in general and individual aspects of it. Such indirectness of expression implies the indirectness and incompleteness of experienced reality itself and, moreover, a corresponding inability of language to represent reality completely. In much of the prose—*Eine Chria,* the correspondence on *Minna von Barnhelm,* and many of the letters to Andres, to name but a few works—and especially in the lyric poetry this experience reveals itself to be primarily of an emotional nature. Indeed, the style emphasizes not so much the object of experience as the experiencing subject. The expression in both prose and poetry may be didactic or expressive, secular or religious, joyful or pessimistic. It may be created by the rationalistic perspectivism of various views, as in the epistles and dialogues in prose and in the didactic poetry, or of disparate realms of experience, as in the lyric. Or it may emerge from the poetic imagery and figures found in both poetry and prose. The objects of experience, the color of the response to them, and the stylistic devices all change. However, the formally and psychologically open structure of experience and the emotionally responsive simple persona remain constant. They are the common denominators of Claudius's uninterpreted works. Claudius is indirect wherever the nature of experienced reality occupies him first and foremost.

The relationship of Claudius's work to experience of a religious kind is observable most clearly, if by no means exclusively, in the prose and poetry where ultimates such as death and transcendence are thematic. A few works, like "Die Mutter am Grabe" and "Der Vater," express immediate experience and certainty of transcendence. More characteristic, however, are *Impetus philosophicus,* "Der Mensch," "Bei ihrem Grabe," and others which manifest an ever-present receptivity to but variously indirect experience of the transcendent. Here, as elsewhere, secular experience, especially physical nature, plays a significant role in perception of the divine. Yet, as Claudius once wrote, man could not draw an analogy to something unseen through the seen if the former were not already within him in some way.[45] Earthly life is for him not the only source of experience, through which one gains a sense of transcendence. It is rather a sensible reminder of another, intangible source of experience, which rests nonetheless within the human soul.

The indirectness of Claudius's work does not signify a devaluation of temporal existence. Far from embracing the asceticism of earlier ages, he was capable of responding with great immediacy to a wide range of earthly experiences and was, by comparison, indeed worldly. On the other hand, it does not betoken atheism either. Claudius always responded to earthly life from a certain distance. Earthly life is important but subordinate to the individual, whose experience is always accessible to and often filled in varying degrees by divinity. Thus, Claudius's gradual, general change to directness does not result from any loss of faith in the world to provide knowledge.[46] For essentials, he never relied on it in the first place, but rather on his own soul.

The presence of interpreted works alongside uninterpreted ones and the intermingling of both modes with varying emphases in others indicates not only the compatibility but also the unity of the two in Claudius's life and work. Both stem from his receptivity to what he perceived as full reality. Where the one stresses the structure of experience, however, the other reflects primarily its content—and Claudius's sense of its importance for all men. The prevalence of direct interpretation in the late work is thus not the consequence of any fundamental change of attitude. It is rather Claudius's way of responding to changes in the times. If much of this late work is less than satisfying aesthetically, it is due to flagging artistic power and to in part intentionally diminished belletristic pretension, not to any grand metamorphosis.

In view of the indirectness of expression and experience over wide areas of Claudius's work, it seems not too much to say that his art is, consciously or unconsciously, a reflection of divine revelation.[47] For in its form, motifs, and general spirit it evinces striking parallels to the Christian God's condescension to man implicit in nature, the Bible, Christ, and other manifestations of sacred history. Just as God's first representative on earth could both embody and spread the word, however, Claudius, too, could raise his forefinger in the gesture of a teacher. In his own unique way Claudius reversed his decision in Jena and became a pastor after all. In the fulfillment of this self-imposed charge lies the broadest sense of his life as the Messenger of Wandsbeck.

Chapter Five
Claudius Today

We have seen that the response to Claudius and his message was highly ambivalent even during his lifetime. Accepted during the 1770s as a highly respected member of the cultural avant-garde, the personal or literary friend of the great as well as a host of minor figures, he was rejected increasingly from the 1780s onward by many of these, as developments in sociopolitical and intellectual history caused a parting of ways. In 1796 Wilhelm von Humboldt could write to the kindred spirit Schiller that he knew nothing at all to say of Claudius, who was, in his view, a complete zero.[1] Some of his old friends and a number of new ones remained receptive to him, however, and when a new historical moment arrived after the turn of the century leading Romantics hailed him as a spiritual father.

Ambivalence has characterized Claudius's reception ever since, again shifting with the flow of the times and attitudes toward politics, philosophy, religion, and art. Claudius's strictly literary influence on later writers has, to all appearances, not been extensive.[2] His greatest influence, on writers and others alike, seems to have been at the level of personal experience, and its extent is thus difficult to determine. In any case the negative criticism has a counterbalance in the homage paid him by many cultural luminaries of the nineteenth and twentieth centuries.

We have already mentioned Eichendorff and Schopenhauer in this connection, each of whom stressed different aspects of the work. Its simplicity moved Schubert to set a number of the poems to music, while its freshness, vividness, and humor inspired Beethoven.[3] In the preface to an anthology Hofmannsthal writes, "Have we selected nothing but great writers? The good Matthias Claudius and Uli Bräker from Toggenburg might be represented as exceptions, but even they are not entirely insignificant: how else could they have been able to assert themselves in the company of the great after one hundred fifty years?"[4] And in another anthology Thomas Mann comments, "But at times something simpler, softer . . . is preferable—whereby Matthias Claudius above all is not to be forgotten with his 'May God watch over this body,' his 'The moon has risen.' . . . In the final analysis nothing surpasses that."[5]

A significant body of devotional writing has grown up around Claudius and continues to be cultivated today, which attests to another kind of highly personal influence. Not surprisingly, his brand of Christian Humanism has had an especially strong appeal during times of crisis. Even scholarly investigation has been most intense in and around the two world wars. Some forty-five studies on various aspects of his life and work were written between 1935 and 1945, for example, at least fourteen in 1940 alone. Dietrich Bonhoeffer, writing in his cell in Tegel, coined the phrase "Christian worldliness" to describe Claudius's approach to life.

Over the past ten to fifteen years there have been signs of a greater willingness to break the silence which has long weighed so heavily over Claudius scholarship. The appearance of the Winkler edition in 1968 and the reprints of *Der Wandsbecker Bote* and the *Hessen-Darmstädtische privilegirte Land-Zeitung* in 1978 mark at least a step in the direction of a truly historical-critical edition of the works. It is to be hoped that Koch and Siebke will fulfill the promise made in their publications of letters in 1972 and 1973.[6] Kranefuß's dissertation of 1973 is currently the most comprehensive and best study of the poetry, while König's dissertation of 1976 represents one of the first serious attempts to view the prose from a specifically literary standpoint. Given all the limitations of Claudius scholarship, Berglar's Rowohlt-monograph of 1972 provides a respectable synthesis. A number of other scholars treated specific problems and works during the 1970s, and Görisch has opened the 1980s with an important dissertation on Claudius's religion and relationship to the *Sturm und Drang.*[7] Claudius's influence on that vast majority of readers who remain silent as a matter of course cannot be measured, but they continue to buy his works.

Despite the vicissitudes of the times and all ambivalence Claudius has been accepted as one of the "classical" writers of German literature. He has even attracted some attention abroad, as close to home as Denmark, Holland, and Italy, and as far away as Japan and America; he has been translated into the languages of these and other countries, including Israel. Yet, the uncertainty of Hofmannsthal's response to his question regarding Claudius's place among German writers suggests the disconcertion with which many still encounter him. This is due at least in part to the remaining confusion over Claudius's literary achievement and relation to his own time and the present. The following summation of the major points made in earlier chapters seeks to respond to this state of affairs.

Judged by the standards of great writers such as Lessing, Wieland, and Goethe, Claudius's production was quite small and his formal and thematic range limited. Throughout his career and especially in his late work he tended toward variation of the congenial rather than toward expansion of his poetic world. Yet, within the given spectrum his diversity is noteworthy. More importantly, he employed prose forms such as the fictional dialogue and correspondence, the feuilleton, and the sermon in a highly original manner and at a level not always attained by more widely recognized authors. In a number of works he exhibits a poetic prose equal or superior to the best of the Rococo writers. He wrung new possibilities of expression from numerous traditional poetic forms, ranging from the verse dialogue and narrative to the cantata. Together with Klopstock and Goethe he brought the folk song and hymn to their highest point in the century. Some of his efforts in these and other genres—"Ein Wiegenlied bei Mondschein zu singen," "Der Tod und das Mädchen," "Der Mensch," "Christiane," "An —— als ihm die —— starb," and "Abendlied," for example—stand among the best of any century or literature.

The warm and at times riotous humor, wit, and irony of both his prose and poetry, placed in the service of humane criticism of human foibles and key issues of the times and life in general, relate Claudius to figures such as Lessing and Wieland, Fielding and Voltaire. He showed signs of developing an entirely new language of satire. His literary criticism in its various forms is surprisingly insightful and on the whole reflective of current judgments. His sense of the dangers inherent in the assumptions regarding human nature which in part led to the French Revolution and the Napoleonic Wars was as keen as Wieland's; in view of the widespread apathy among the German cultural elite during this period his continued engagement is remarkable.

The possibility and nature of human knowledge were among Claudius's central concerns, which led him to devote much of his essayistic work to the epistemological controversy in the theology and philosophy of the century. If derived from the traditional Protestant view, his attitude exerted as formative an influence on his belletristic work as that of the more secular Wieland; perspectivism, manifesting the relativity of all temporal knowledge, characterizes much of his poetry and prose.

Significant elements of the rationalism of the age enter into harmony with Christian irrationalism in Claudius's life and work. The complementary if unequal roles of intuition or spirit and reason are apparent in his epistemology, poetics, and the fusion of expressivity and didacticism in much of his poetry and prose. The unity of his experience, thought, and work is all the more notable for its rarity. If always proceeding from and returning to Christianity, Claudius in a sense had the best of all worlds. He organically assimilated the mixture of the cheerful and the earnest, the formally complete and fragmentary, and the prose and poetry of the Rococo, avoiding its coldness and intellectualism; the warmth and realism of Sentimentalism, shunning its excesses; and the sense of the mission of art of the Classicists and Romantics, eschewing their self-sufficiency and complacency.

Claudius's motifs were few, but to a large extent universal. Indeed, his greatest achievement lies in his ability to communicate his own experience of these universals in such a way as to re-create similar experience in the reader. In this respect he transcends time and place. His expressions of childlike wonder, joy, and sorrow before these basics of life at levels accessible to adults and children alike are reminiscent of Hans Christian Andersen.

As a religious writer Claudius was at once a consistent humanist and Protestant. Along with other artists of the reform-minded century he reveals a deep concern for the material and psychological well-being of his fellows. The common good of mankind entailed for him, unlike many, however, a spiritual dimension, and he never tired of impressing upon his readers the importance of his, on the whole, liberal interpretation of Luther's religion in all phases of life. Due to his own experience and, in part, very literal acceptance of Luther he was keenly aware of man's difference and essential isolation from God, of his existence in the original sense of the word, to step or stand out. This awareness caused him considerable torment, which could be only partially alleviated by his very real faith and moments of certainty. Claudius's *experience* of transcendence was that of Søren Kierkegaard and Karl Barth, if not as uniformly anguished as the former's or as positive regarding faith as the latter's. Like Karl Jaspers, he turned to the various ciphers of transcendence concealed in the world of past and present. More consistently, however, he sought them within his own soul. Perhaps as adamantly as any writer during his own time or since he rejected the gnostic heresy, which in its broad interpretation and various forms, according to Eric Voegelin, has characterized the West increasingly since the Middle Ages.[8]

Readers who require of literature novel expressions of great ideas may well close Claudius's work disappointed. In terms of basic human experience, whether worldly or religious, however, he can still speak today to those in Germany and abroad who have an ear for his message.

Notes and References

Preface

1. Annelen Kranefuß, *Die Gedichte des Wandsbecker Boten* (Göttingen, 1973); Burghard König, *Matthias Claudius: Die literarischen Beziehungen im Leben und Werk* (Bonn, 1976).

2. See Jeffrey L. Sammons's review of William J. Lillyman, *Reality's Dark Dream: The Narrative Fiction of Ludwig Tieck,* in *German Quarterly* 52 (1979): 544–45.

3. T. S. Eliot, "What Is Minor Poetry?", in his *On Poetry and Poets* (New York: Farrar, Straus and Cudahy, 1957), pp. 34–51.

4. J. Max Patrick, "Introduction," *The Complete Poetry of Robert Herrick* (New York: Norton, 1968), p. vii.

Chapter One

1. For the general information in this chapter I am indebted to the following sources: Wilhelm Herbst, *Matthias Claudius der Wandsbecker Bote: Ein deutsches Stillleben,* 4th ed. (Gotha, 1878); Carl Mönckeberg, *Matthias Claudius: Ein Beitrag zur Kirchen- und Litterar-Geschichte seiner Zeit* (Hamburg, 1869); Wolfgang Stammler, *Matthias Claudius der Wandsbecker Bothe: Ein Beitrag zur deutschen Literatur- und Geistesgeschichte* (Halle, 1915); Urban Roedl, *Matthias Claudius: Sein Weg und seine Welt* (Hamburg, 1969); Peter Berglar, *Matthias Claudius* (Reinbek bei Hamburg, 1972). I, of course, am responsible for the interpretation of the material. I will limit references to these works to matters of special importance.

2. See "Der nützliche Gelehrte," "Eine Chria," and "Eine Disputation," *Matthias Claudius: Sämtliche Werke,* ed. Jost Perfahl, Wolfgang Pfeiffer-Belli, and Hansjörg Platschek (Munich, 1972), pp. 724, 19, and 60, respectively.

3. Most commentators acknowledge the significance of this experience in Claudius's development but do not clearly recognize the spiritual-intellectual dilemma it placed before him and the likely consequences of his attempt to resolve it.

4. *Sämtliche Werke,* pp. 887–94.

5. See, for example, Herbst, *Matthias Claudius,* p. 39, and Roedl, *Matthias Claudius,* p. 24. The doubt is expressed in each case with little or no substantiation.

6. *Sämtliche Werke,* p. 892.

7. Ibid, p. 888.

8. "An eine Quelle," ibid., pp. 708, 69.

9. See "Ich mag heut nicht im Dichterschmuck erscheinen" and "Der nützliche Gelehrte," ibid., pp. 725, 724, respectively.

10. See, for example, Herbst, *Matthias Claudius,* pp. 4–5, and Stammler, *Matthias Claudius,* pp. 26–27.

11. See Walter Bruford, *Germany in the Eighteenth Century: The Social Background of the Literary Revival* (Cambridge: At the University Press, 1965), pp. 271–90.

12. See Claudius's letter to Gerstenberg of 2 October 1763, Matthias Claudius, *Botengänge: Briefe an Freunde,* ed. Hans Jessen, 2d ed. (Berlin, 1965), p. 20. For the other five see pp. 14–20.

13. Extremely little is known of his activity there. Even the Dane Richard Petersen is unable to shed any light in his lengthy, little-known study, *Matthias Claudius og Hans Vennekreds* (Copenhagen, 1884).

14. Helmut de Boor and Richard Newald, *Geschichte der deutschen Literatur von den Anfängen bis zur Gegenwart* (Munich: C. H. Beck' sche Verlagsbuchhandlung, 1957), Vol. I, part I, p. 25.

15. Roedl, *Matthias Claudius,* p. 37.

16. *Sämtliche Werke,* p. 26.

17. See, for example, "Impetus philosophicus," ibid., pp. 817–18, which is discussed in the present study beginning on p. 71.

18. The definitive study of the literary influences on Claudius remains to be written. If and when it appears, it will almost certainly emphasize Claudius's fundamental independence. Hamann would seem to have been an important model for him, yet Kranefuß denies any true influence, *Die Gedichte,* pp. 221–23.

19. Wolfgang Martens, *Die Botschaft der Tugend: Die Aufklärung im Spiegel der deutschen Moralischen Wochenschriften* (Stuttgart: Metzler, 1968). See especially Part I in this connection.

20. 7 June 1770, *Botengänge,* p. 64.

21. 28 October 1770, ibid., p. 68.

22. See Carl Redlich, *Die poetischen Beiträge zum Wandsbecker Bothen, gesammelt und ihren Verfassern zugewiesen* (Hamburg, 1871), pp. 59–60.

23. Roedl, *Matthias Claudius,* p. 76.

24. *Sämtliche Werke,* p. 779.

25. The name "Asmus" first appears in no. 133 of 1771, not in no. 98 of 1774, as the editors of the *Sämtliche Werke* state (p. 997). Their mistake may rest on that of Stammler, *Matthias Claudius,* p. 91. See *Der Wandsbecker Bote,* ed. Karl Heinrich Rengstorf and Hans-Albrecht Koch (Wandsbeck, 1771; rpt. Hildesheim, 1978).

26. Claudius's critics have continually failed to distinguish clearly among these personae. This has led to a lack of clarity regarding the role of each and of the fictional circle as a whole.

27. *Sämtliche Werke,* pp. 50, 125, respectively.

28. Ibid., pp. 35, 78, 108, 152.

29. Ibid., pp. 44 and 792.

30. Rolf Christian Zimmermann is one of the most recent contributors to the Claudius myth: "Matthias Claudius," in: *Deutsche Dichter des 18. Jahrhunderts: Ihr Leben und Werk,* ed. Benno von Wiese (Berlin, 1977).

31. To Gerstenberg, 3 September 1771, and to Herder, 20 September 1771, *Botengänge,* pp. 78–80.

32. See undated letter to Herder, ibid., pp. 85–86.

33. See Stammler, *Matthias Claudius,* p. 230, note 11.

34. Berglar, *Matthias Claudius,* p. 99.

35. Stammler, for example, entitles his chapter on this period "Wandsbeck Still Life 1770–76."

36. See, for example, the letters to Voβ, January 1775, and undated, *Botengänge,* pp. 124, 126, respectively.

37. Perusal of the inclusive dates of publication of the many papers listed by Martens, *Die Botschaft der Tugend,* pp. 544–55, provides ample evidence of the relatively long life of Claudius's paper.

38. Undated letter to Herder, *Botengänge,* p. 80.

39. *Sämtliche Werke,* p. 11.

40. Ibid. "Ruprecht Pförtner" is apparently a humorous folk name for a doorkeeper.

41. Quoted according to Stammler, *Matthias Claudius,* p. 129. For a similar statement by another contemporary, see Herbst, *Matthias Claudius,* 3d ed. (Gotha, 1863), pp. 275, and 592–93.

42. Letter to Herder, 5 December 1775, *Botengänge,* p. 178. Commentators have frequently abused the identity of man and writer in Claudius. However, the attempts to explain it away have often been equally abusive. Kranefuβ's explanation of Claudius's comment to Herder (*Die Gedichte,* pp. 9–11), for example, completely ignores the context in which it was made. My understanding of this identity is elucidated in the first section of Chapter 3 of this study.

43. *Sämtliche Werke,* p. 599.

44. Stammler, *Matthias Claudius,* pp. 96–98.

45. 10 August 1776, *Botengänge,* p. 207.

46. *Hessen-Darmstädtische privilegirte Land-Zeitung 1777: Faksimileausgabe des von Matthias Claudius redigierten Teils und Nachlese aus dem ersten Jahrgang (1777),* ed. Jörg-Ulrich Fechner (Darmstadt, 1978).

47. A. Meier provides information about this and other such unsubstantiated claims in "Abendlied des Matthias Claudius," *Der Wandsbeker,* September 1953, pp. 9–10.

48. See undated letter to Moser, *Botengänge,* pp. 230–33.

49. See "Nachwort," *Land-Zeitung,* pp. 238–39.

50. See note 48.

51. See "Nachwort," *Land-Zeitung,* pp. 268–69.

52. Ibid., pp. 269–70.

53. *Sämtliche Werke,* p. 162.

54. Claudius's words "Befiehl Du Deine Wege" ("Commit thy way") represent a variation on Psalms 37:5 and Luther's version composed by the seventeenth-century poet Paul Gerhardt and included in Protestant prayer books.

55. See "Slaegten Claudius," *Saertryk af Personalhistorisk Tidsskrift* 3–4 (1943): 187–207.

56. See, for example, Zimmermann, *Deutsche Dichter,* pp. 438–39, and König, *Die literarischen Beziehungen,* in numerous passages.

57. Terrasson, *Geschichte des Ägyptischen Königs Sethos* (Breslau: Löwe, 1777–1778); Ramsay, *Die Reisen des Cyrus: eine moralische Geschichte* (Breslau: Löwe, 1780); Saint Martin, *Irrthümer und Wahrheit* (Breslau: Löwe, 1782); Fénelon, *Fénelons Werke religiösen Inhalts,* 3 vols. (Hamburg: Perthes, 1800, 1809, and 1811). The third volume of the translation of Fénelon contains a selection of Pascal's *Pensées sur la religion* in translation.

58. See John A. McCarthy, "Wielands Metamorphose" *Deutsche Vierteljahresschrift für Literaturgeschichte* 49 (1975): 149–67. "Sonderheft, 18. Jahrhundert."

59. Friedrich Loofs, *Matthias Claudius in kirchengeschichtlicher Beleuchtung: Eine Untersuchung über Claudius' religiöse Stellung und Altersentwicklung* (Gotha, 1915). Hans-Albrecht Koch and Rolf Siebke are among the few who have pointed to Loofs and attempted to debunk this aspect of the myth, "Unbekannte Briefe und Texte von Matthias Claudius nebst einigen Bemerkungen zur Claudius-Forschung," *Jahrbuch des Freien Deutschen Hochstifts,* 1972, pp. 1–35.

60. Undated, *Botengänge,* p. 102.

61. Roedl, *Matthias Claudius,* pp. 72–73.

62. Loofs, *Matthias Claudius,* pp. 87–89.

63. *Sämtliche Werke,* p. 596.

64. See Gregor Sebba, "Order and Disorders of the Soul: Eric Voegelin's Philosophy of History," *Southern Review,* n.s. 3 (1967): 282–86.

65. *Sämtliche Werke,* pp. 416, 370, respectively.

66. Ibid., pp. 938–46.

67. See, for example, "Briefe an Andres," "Brief an Andres," "Das heilige Abendmahl," "Vom Gewissen," "Vom Vaterunser," and "Geburt und Wiedergeburt," ibid., pp. 477, 367, 607, 677, 641, 659, respectively.

68. Ibid., pp. 545, 573, respectively.

69. "Brief des Pythagoreers Lysias an den Hipparchus," "Sprüche des Pythagoreers Demophilus," "Das Gebet," "Über die Unsterblichkeit der Seele," "Uber die Glückseligkeit: Krischna," "Hauptpunkte der von Holl-well bekanntgemachten Fragmente des Schasta," ibid., pp. 671, 674, 218, 474, 475, 475 respectively.

70. Ibid., p. 499. Christel Matthias Schröder places this work in its historical context in *Matthias Claudius und die Religionsgeschichte,* 2d ed. (Hamburg: Dulk, 1948).

71. "Auf O--o R--s Grab," *Sämtliche Werke,* p. 623.

72. Anne Louise Germaine de Staël-Holstein, *De l'Allemagne* (London: J. Murray, 1813).

73. Herbst, *Matthias Claudius,* 4th ed., p. 247.

74. Ibid. Both incidents were reported by Friedrich von Matthisson.

75. See note 55.

76. Mönckeberg, *Matthias Claudius,* pp. 382–93.

77. See Clemens Theodor Perthes, *Friedrich Perthes' Leben nach dessen schriftlichen und mündlichen Mittheilungen,* 6th ed., 3 vols. in 1 (Gotha: Perthes, 1872), 2:48.

Chapter Two

1. See Loofs, *Matthias Claudius,* especially pp. 11–12, 22–28, 41–49, 117–44.

2. See "Vom Gewissen" and "Valet an meine Leser," *Sämtliche Werke,* pp. 679, 601–2, respectively.

3. See "Von und mit," ibid., pp. 393–99, and the letters to Jacobi, *Botengänge,* pp. 372, 379, 382.

4. See "Eine asiatische Vorlesung" and "Nachricht von meiner Audienz beim Kaiser von Japan," *Sämtliche Werke,* pp. 531, 140, respectively.

5. See the reviews of Herder's *Älteste Urkunde des Menschengeschlechts* and Goethe's *Zwo wichtige biblische Fragen* as well as "Übungen im Stil" and "Briefe an Andres," ibid., pp. 35–38, 837–38, 467, 482–84, respectively.

6. See "Einfältiger Hausvater-Bericht" and the review of *Die Taufe der Christen,* ibid., pp. 573, 862–63, respectively.

7. "Einfältiger Hausvater-Bericht," ibid., p. 592.

8. "Hinz und Kunz" and the review of *Neue Apologie des Sokrates,* ibid., p. 791, the corresponding note on p. 1045, and pp. 22–23, respectively. The question was then very current.

9. See the review of *Hirtenbrief S. H. G. des Bischofs von Speyer an seine Geistliche* and "Das heilige Abendmahl," ibid., pp. 822, 615–17, respectively.

10. See "Zwei Rezensionen etc. in Sachen der Herren Lessing, M. Mendelssohn, und Jacobi" and the review of *Anleitung über die Religion vernünftig zu denken,* ibid., pp. 348–60, 813, respectively.

11. Johann Heinrich Voß, "Wie ward Fritz Stolberg ein Unfreier?," *Voß: Werke in einem Band,* ed. Hedwig Voegt (Berlin and Weimar: Aufbau, 1966), pp. 293–395, and *Bestätigung der Stolbergischen Umtriebe, nebst einem Anhang über persönliche Verhältnisse* (Stuttgart: Metzler, 1820); see also portions of letters from Jacobi to Stolberg in Roedl, *Matthias Claudius,* pp. 297–98.

12. Dietrich Bonhoeffer, *Widerstand und Ergebung: Briefe und Aufzeichnungen aus der Haft,* ed. Eberhard Bethge, 2d ed. (Munich: Kaiser, 1970), p. 257f.

13. See "Über die Unsterblichkeit der Seele," "Zwei Rezensionen," "Von und mit," and "Über einige Sprüche des Prediger Salomo," *Sämtliche Werke,* pp. 286, 357–58, 397, 245–46, respectively.

14. See "Morgengespräch zwischen A. und dem Kandidaten Bertram," ibid., p. 654.

15. "Zwei Rezensionen," ibid., p. 357.

16. "Eine Abhandlung vom menschlichen Herzen, *sehr kurios zu lesen,*" ibid., pp. 760–63.

17. "Übungen im Stil," ibid., p. 462.

18. "Morgengespräch" and "Geburt und Wiedergeburt," ibid., pp. 654, 659–61, respectively.

19. See, for example, the reviews of *Philosophie der Religion* and *Discours sur les fruits des bonnes études,* ibid., pp. 826, 56–57, respectively.

20. "Morgengespräch," ibid., p. 649.

21. Ibid., p. 149.

22. Ibid., pp. 207–8.

23. Ibid., p. 447.

24. Ibid., pp. 16–17.

25. Ibid., pp. 257–59.

26. See, for example, "Parentation über Anselmo, *gehalten am ersten Weihnachttage,*" ibid., pp. 177–78.

27. Ibid., pp. 259–61.

28. Rolf Siebke, "Arthur Schopenhauer und Matthias Claudius," *Schopenhauer-Jahrbuch* 51 (1970): 24–25.

29. "Morgengespräch," *Sämtliche Werke,* pp. 654–57.

30. "Was ich wohl mag," ibid., p. 17.

31. Ibid., p. 178.

32. Ibid., p. 716.

33. "An S. bei — Begräbnis," ibid., p. 80.

34. Gotthold Ephraim Lessing, *Sämtliche Schriften,* ed. Karl Lachmann & Franz Muncker, 3d ed. (Stuttgart: Göschen, 1895), 11:55.

35. Johann Gottfried Herder, *Sämmtliche Werke,* ed. Bernhard Suphan (Berlin: Weidmann, 1891), 5:656.

36. "Über einige Sprüche des Prediger Salomo," *Sämtliche Werke,* p. 242.

37. See Zimmermann, *Deutsche Dichter,* p. 440.

38. This is part of a phrase made famous by Conrad Ferdinand Meyer, who included it in the motto to his *Huttens letzte Tage.*

39. *Sämtliche Werke,* p. 44.

40. Ibid., pp. 57, 84, 87.

41. Ibid., pp. 806–7.

42. Ibid., p. 25.

43. Ibid., pp. 220–22.

44. Ibid., p. 579.

45. Ibid., pp. 473–74.

46. Ibid., p. 128.

47. Examples of such distortions are found in Hans Jessen and Ernst Schröder, "Einleitung," *Matthias Claudius: Asmus und die Seinen, Briefe an die Familie* (Berlin, 1940), pp. 5–16; F. J. Curt Hoefer, "Der Wandsbecker Bothe: Ein Beitrag zur Geschichte der Deutschen Publizistik des 18. Jahrhunderts," Ph.D. diss., Leipzig, 1944; and Günter Albrecht, "Einleitung," *Werke des Wandsbecker Boten* (Schwerin: Petermänken, 1958), 1:9–50, especially p. 32.

48. *Herders Sämmtliche Werke,* 5:475.

49. *Sämtliche Werke,* pp. 108–9.

50. Ibid., p. 83.

51. Ibid., pp. 639–40.

52. Ibid., p. 514.

53. This is especially true of "Eine asiatische Vorlesung" and "Über die neue Politik," ibid., pp. 499–535, 416–43, respectively.

54. Ibid., pp. 144–45.

55. Ibid., pp. 294–310.

56. Ibid., pp. 119–24.

57. Ibid., p. 143.

58. Ibid., p. 236.

59. Ibid., p. 218.

60. Ibid., p. 230.

61. See "Schreiben eines Dänen an seinen Freund," ibid., pp. 959–62, which Claudius wrote in response to the English blockade of Danish ports in 1807.

62. William Flint Thrall, Addison Hibbard, and C. Hugh Holman, *A Handbook to Literature,* rev. ed. (New York: Odyssey, 1960), p. 448.

63. The work appears in altered form in the *Sämtliche Werke,* pp. 25–26.

64. Ibid., p. 25.

65. Ibid.

66. Ibid., pp. 50–53.

67. Ibid., p. 51.

68. Ibid.

69. Ibid., pp. 46–49.

70. Ibid., p. 851.

71. See "An den Naber mit Rat," ibid., pp. 951–58.

72. Ibid., p. 25.

73. Ibid., p. 136.

74. Ibid., p. 70.

75. Ibid., p. 647.

76. Ibid., p. 648.

77. Letter to Herder, 18 April 1776, *Botengänge,* p. 193.

78. *Sämtliche Werke,* pp. 887, 725.

79. Ibid., p. 367.

80. See the review of Herder's *Abhandlung über den Ursprung der Sprache,* ibid., pp. 78–80, where Claudius agrees largely with his friend's pertinent remarks on language.

81. Ibid., p. 319. Also see p. 881.

82. Ibid., pp. 225–26.

83. Ibid., pp. 792–95, 44–45.

84. See the reviews of Friedrich Nicolai's satire of *Werther* in *Freuden des jungen Werthers* and of the attack on Goethe's critics in Heinrich Leopold Wagner's *Prometheus, Deukalion und seine Rezensenten,* ibid., pp. 876, 877, respectively; also see the works from p. 938 to p. 946.

85. Ibid., pp. 881–82, 90–92, respectively.

86. Ibid., p. 819.

87. William Wimsatt, *The Verbal Icon: Studies in the Meaning of Poetry* (Lexington: University of Kentucky Press, 1954), pp. 21–39.

88. *Sämtliche Werke,* p. 606.

89. Ibid., p. 599.

Chapter Three

1. Zimmermann, *Deutsche Dichter,* p. 441.

2. Jörg Schönert, *Roman und Satire im 18. Jahrhundert: ein Beitrag zur Poetik* (Stuttgart: Metzler, 1969).

3. Goethe describes his work as "fragments of a great confession" in the seventh book of *Dichtung und Wahrheit.*

4. Martens, *Die Botschaft der Tugend,* pp. 29–99.

5. See Lieselotte E. Kurth-Voigt, *Perspectives and Points of View: The Early Works of Wieland and Their Background* (Baltimore and London: Johns Hopkins University Press, 1974).

6. *Sämtliche Werke,* p. 95.

7. Ibid., pp. 12–13.

8. For example, "Der Küster Christen Ahrendt," "Politische Korrespondenz zwischen dem Küster Ahrendt und dem Verwalter Olufsen," "Von und mit," "An den Naber mit Rat," "Schreiben eines Dänen," and "Predigt eines Laienbruders," ibid., pp. 902, 913, 370, 951, 959, 691, respectively.

9. Cf. the first, second, fourth, and fifth works in the preceding note.

10. See, for example, the *Brief an Andres,* ibid., pp. 666–70. In religious and some literary circles Claudius is best known for such works, which are highly successful in their kind. In them he strikes a compromise between the language of emotion and everyday language.

11. Alfred Anger, *Literarisches Rokoko,* 2d ed. (Stuttgart: Metzler, 1968), pp. 52–54.

12. One important prose work is not discussed here due to space restrictions and my extensive treatment of it elsewhere. "Paul Erdmanns Fest," *Sämtliche Werke,* pp. 188–212, which represents Claudius's definitive poetic expression of his views on society and politics and discloses his most typical handling of the dramatic narrative, is the subject of "Matthias Claudius's *Paul Erdmanns Fest* and the Utopian Tradition," *Seminar* 18 (1982): 14–26.

13. Ibid., pp. 19–21.

14. Ibid., p. 19.

15. Ibid., pp. 19–20.

16. Ibid., p. 20.

17. Ibid.

18. Ibid.

19. Ibid.

20. Ibid., p. 21.

21. Ibid.

22. Ibid., p. 19.

23. The title continues whimsically "Who in His Whole Life Had Never Seen a River Other Than the River Essiquebo on Which He Lived," ibid., pp. 737–39.

24. Ibid., p. 738.

25. Ibid., p. 739.

26. See the entry on "Schlittschuh" in Friedrich Kluge and Alfred

Götze, *Etymologisches Wörterbuch der deutschen Sprache,* 16th ed. (Berlin: de Gruyter, 1953), p. 675.

27. *The Odes and Epodes of Horace: A Modern English Verse Translation,* tr. Joseph P. Clancy (Chicago: University of Chicago Press, 1960), p. 104.

28. *Goethes Werke,* Hamburger Ausgabe, 10:61–63, and *Etymologisches Wörterbuch,* p. 675.

29. *Sämtliche Werke,* pp. 111–12.

30. Ibid., p. 111.

31. Ibid.

32. Ibid.

33. Ibid., pp. 111–12.

34. Ibid., p. 112.

35. Ibid., pp. 757–58.

36. Ibid.

37. See Schönert, *Roman und Satire,* p. 73.

38. *Sämtliche Werke,* p. 54.

39. Ibid.

40. Ibid.

41. Ibid., pp. 817–18.

42. Ibid. *Barbara celarent* are the first two in a long series of unconnected words which in classical Rome served to help students of philosophy to memorize the principles of logic. See Heinrich G. Reichert, *Urban und Human: Unvergängliche lateinische Spruchweisheit* (Munich: Goldmann, 1965), pp. 218–23, especially p. 221.

43. *Sämtliche Werke,* p. 1044.

44. Ibid.

45. Ibid., pp. 749–57.

46. Ibid., p. 749.

47. Ibid., p. 750.

48. Ibid.

49. Ibid., p. 751.

50. Ibid., pp. 750–51.

51. Ibid., pp. 751–52.

52. Ibid., p. 752.

53. Ibid., p. 753.

54. Ibid., p. 754.

55. In his first letter Fritz writes, "Often I had spots before my eyes and I thought there would be some dead people, but everything turned out all right, thank God," ibid., p. 751.

Chapter Four

1. Herbert A. and Elisabeth Frenzel, *Daten deutscher Dichtung: Chron-*

ologischer Abriß der deutschen Literaturgeschichte von den Anfängen bis zur Gegenwart, 6th ed. (Munich: DTV, 1970), vol. 1.

2. The classification generally follows that of Kranefuß, *Die Gedichte des Wandsbecker Boten.* Here, as elsewhere in this chapter, my indebtedness to this excellent study is manifest. The resemblances as well as the differences stem to a considerable extent, however, from similar but independent readings of Claudius.

3. Ibid., p. 87.

4. *Sämtliche Werke,* p. 23.

5. Ibid., p. 58.

6. Ibid., pp. 815–17.

7. They also state views on, among other subjects, philosophy and morality, ibid., pp. 89, 163, 898, 899.

8. Ibid., p. 95.

9. Ibid., p. 84.

10. Ibid., pp. 449–50.

11. Stammler, *Matthias Claudius,* p. 170.

12. *Sämtliche Werke,* pp. 17–18.

13. Ibid., pp. 543–44.

14. Ibid., pp. 548, 550, respectively.

15. Ibid., pp. 126–27. See König, *Die literarischen Beziehungen,* pp. 258–61.

16. *Sämtliche Werke,* pp. 109–10.

17. Ibid., pp. 363, 675, 467, respectively.

18. Ibid., p. 457. The poem was probably dedicated to Frau Schimmelmann.

19. Ibid., p. 174.

20. Ibid., p. 33.

21. Ibid., p. 124.

22. Ibid., p. 92.

23. Goethe's work, *The Triumph of Sentimentality,* satirized the excesses of emotionalism.

24. *Sämtliche Werke,* pp. 84–85.

25. Kranefuß compiles a list of adjectives appearing in the nature poems which indicate the emotionalization of the experience of nature, *Die Gedichte des Wandsbecker Boten,* pp. 137–38.

26. Kranefuß overlooks or underestimates such poems in Chapter 5 of her book, where she stresses the "friendliness of nature," ibid., pp. 123–46. Her emphasis stems from her basic attempt to account for the realism of Claudius's work, which is indeed greater than in the work of most "Christian" or "religious" poets and which she sees as related to the eighteenth-century process of secularization. An adequate response to this aspect of her quite systematic argument cannot be made here, although it should be borne in mind that this and other sections of the present

study represent a reaction to her general argument. Suffice it to say here that her concept of reality tends to exclude or at least devalue spiritual reality, which for Claudius was always of the utmost essence, and that the worldliness of the Old Testament, Luther, and Claudius, which could be pessimistic as well as optimistic, measures itself on the reality of spirit.

27. *Sämtliche Werke,* pp. 235–36.

28. Ibid., p. 473.

29. J. Carl Ernst Sommer, *Studien zu den Gedichten des Wandsbecker Boten* (Frankfurt am Main, 1935, rpt. Hildesheim, 1973), p. 51.

30. *Sämtliche Werke,* p. 1066. The musical adaptations of this and other poems are listed by Max Friedländer, *Das deutsche Lied im 18. Jahrhundert: Quellen und Studien* (Stuttgart & Berlin, 1902), 2:244–59.

31. *Sämtliche Werke,* pp. 75–77.

32. Ibid., p. 248.

33. Kranefuß, *Die Gedichte des Wandsbecker Boten,* pp. 195–96.

34. *Sämtliche Werke,* pp. 149–50.

35. Ibid., pp. 86–87.

36. First by Sommer, *Studien,* p. 46, and later with greater detail by Kranefuß, *Die Gedichte des Wandsbecker Boten,* pp. 159–61. For a discussion of the controversy surrounding the change in the third line of the maiden's strophe in the second version see Kranefuß, p. 160, note 28.

37. The comma after *nicht* represents more a grammatical than a rhythmical caesura.

38. See Ferdinand Naumann, *Matthias Claudius und das Volkslied* Ph.D. diss., Greifswald, 1914, p. 57, with whom Kranefuß seems to concur, *Die Gedichte des Wandsbecker Boten,* p. 162.

39. "Bei dem Grabe Anselmos" may have been written on the death of his first child at birth in 1772, *Sämtliche Werke,* pp. 21, 1001.

40. Ibid., p. 473. In addition to being set to music a number of times, the poem was included in Clemens Brentano and Achim von Arnim's famous collection of folk songs *Des Knaben Wunderhorn,* ibid., p. 1034.

41. Ibid., p. 938.

42. Ibid., p. 279.

43. The possible reading of the fifth line as a result clause would not essentially alter the meaning of the poem.

44. *Sämtliche Werke,* p. 217.

45. Ibid., pp. 285–87.

46. Kranefuß, *Die Gedichte des Wandsbecker Boten,* p. 191.

47. Ibid., especially Chapters 7 and 8.

Chapter Five

1. Letter from Schiller to Goethe, 23 November 1796, *Schillers Briefe,* ed. Fritz Jonas (Stuttgart: Deutsche Verlagsanstalt, 1895), 5:91.

2. Stammler, *Matthias Claudius,* provides a brief overview, pp. 210–11.

3. See Dietrich Fischer-Dieskau, *Auf den Spuren der Schubert-Lieder: Werden–Wesen–Wirkung* (Munich: DTV, 1976), pp. 103–4, and Friedländer, *Das deutsche Lied.*

4. Hugo von Hofmannsthal, *Gesammelte Werke in Einzelausgaben* (Frankfurt am Main: S. Fischer, 1966), Prosa IV, 133.

5. Thomas Mann, *Gesammelte Werke in 13 Bänden* (Frankfurt am Main: S. Fischer, 1974), 10:922.

6. Hans-Albrecht Koch and Rolf Siebke, "Unbekannte Briefe und Texte von Matthias Claudius nebst einigen Bemerkungen zur Claudius-Forschung," *Jahrbuch des Freien Deutschen Hochstifts,* 1972, pp. 1–35, and "Nachträge zu 'Unbekannte Briefe und Texte von Matthias Claudius,' " *Jahrbuch des Freien Deutschen Hochstifts,* 1973, pp. 481–83.

7. Karl Heinrich Rengstorf discusses Claudius's humanism in "Humanität und Inhumanität bei Matthias Claudius," *Wolfenbüttler Studien zur Aufklärung* 3 (1976): 227–57; Jörg-Ulrich Fechner treats him in connection with literary sociology in "Matthias Claudius und die Literatursoziologie?," *Geist und Zeichen: Festschrift für Arthur Henkel zu seinem 60. Geburtstag,* ed. Herbert Anton, Bernhard Gajek, and Peter Pfaff (Heidelberg, 1977), pp. 57–74; Rolf Eigenwald presents a long discussion of "Abendlied" in "Matthias Claudius und sein 'Abendlied,' " *Projekt Deutschunterricht* 9 (1975), pp. 177–201; Georg-Michael Schulz has discussed "Abendlied" more recently in "Matthias Claudius' 'Abendlied.' Kreatürlichkeit und Aufklärungskritik," *Deutsche Vierteljahresschrift für Literatur und Geistesgeschichte* 53 (1979), 233–50; and Reinhold Görisch studies Claudius's relationship to the *Sturm und Drang* in *Matthias Claudius und der Sturm und Drang* (Frankfurt am Main, 1981).

8. Eric Voegelin, *The New Science of Politics: An Introduction* (Chicago and London: University of Chicago Press, 1952).

Selected Bibliography

Due to space restrictions this bibliography is limited mainly to works which were especially helpful in the preparation of this study. Both in agreement and disagreement I am indebted to them and a number of other studies not included here. There is unfortunately no comprehensive critical bibliography on Claudius.

PRIMARY SOURCES

1. Works

Asmus omnia sua secum portans, oder Sämmtliche Werke des Wandsbecker Bothen, I. und II. Theil. Hamburg: Bode, 1775.

III. Theil. Breslau: Löwe, 1778.

IV. Theil. Breslau: Löwe, 1783.

V. Theil. Hamburg: Bohn, 1790.

VI. Theil. Hamburg: Perthes, 1798.

VII. Theil. Hamburg: Perthes, 1803.

VIII. Theil. Hamburg: The Author, 1812.

Matthias Claudius: Werke. Edited by Carl Christian Redlich. 10th ed., 2 vols. in 1. Gotha: Perthes, 1879. The best of the nineteenth-century editorial efforts. All subsequent editions are identical with this one.

Matthias Claudius' ausgewählte Werke. Edited by Wilhelm Flegler. Leipzig: Reclam, 1882. Valuable mainly for its annotations.

Matthias Claudius' Werke. Edited by Georg Behrmann. Leipzig: Hesse, 1907. Arranged chronologically rather than according to the volumes of *Asmus,* the edition complements others by providing a greater sense of the continuity of Claudius's writing.

Matthias Claudius: Sämtliche Werke. Edited by Jost Perfahl, Wolfgang Pfeiffer-Belli, and Hansjörg Platschek. Munich: Winkler, 1968. This edition follows the text of the first editions and is the most complete to date. It also offers one of the lengthiest bibliographies available, pp. 1057–67. However, it still contains lacunae, the afterword leaves much to be desired, and the commentary, most unfortunately, leaves much to the imagination. The plates, separated from the corresponding texts, lose most of their impact.

2. Newspapers

Hamburger Adreβ-Comptoir-Nachrichten. Located, with certain missing numbers, in the Staats- und Universitätsbibliothek in Hamburg. The absence of a reprint edition is compensated for in part by the inclusion of the literary works in the Winkler edition.

Der Wandsbecker Bothe. Edited by Karl Heinrich Rengstorf and Hans-Albrecht Koch. 5 vols. Hildesheim: Olms, 1978.

Hessen-Darmstädtische privilegirte Land-Zeitung: Faksimileausgabe des von Matthias Claudius redigierten Teils und Nachlese aus dem ersten Jahrgang (1777). Edited by Jörg-Ulrich Fechner. Darmstadt: Roether, 1978. The text and extensive afterword provide insight into Claudius's personal life and sociopolitical and journalistic activity in Darmstadt as well as general information on the journalism and politics of the time.

3. Correspondence

Matthias Claudius: Botengänge, Briefe an Freunde. Edited by Hans Jessen. 2d ed. Berlin: Eckart, 1965. The most complete collection of Claudius's letters to his friends. It is far from exhaustive, however, offers many in abridged form, and provides an unreliable and very limited commentary.

Matthias Claudius und die Seinen: Briefe. Vol. 2. Edited by Hans Jessen and Ernst Schröder. Berlin: Eckart, 1940. While the most complete edition of Claudius's letters to his family, the collection suffers from the deficiencies mentioned above.

Matthias Claudius schreibt an die Seinen: Familienbriefe. Edited by Hans Jürgen Schultz. Witten and Berlin: Eckart, 1955. A far shorter version of the previous work with no commentary but containing a few previously unpublished letters.

Koch, Hans-Albrecht, and Siebke, Rolf. "Unbekannte Briefe und Texte von Matthias Claudius nebst einigen Bemerkungen zur Claudius-Forschung." *Jahrbuch des Freien Deutschen Hochstifts,* 1972, pp. 1–35. Contains previously unpublished letters as well as bibliographical material and a discussion of some of the current problems in Claudius studies.

———. "Nachträge zu 'Unbekannte Briefe und Texte von Matthias Claudius.' " *Jahrbuch des Freien Deutschen Hochstifts,* 1973, pp. 481–83.

SECONDARY SOURCES

Berglar, Peter. *Matthias Claudius in Selbstzeugnissen und Bilddokumenten.* Reinbek bei; Hamburg: Rowohlt, 1972. A brief but useful introduction to the life and work, which contains a valuable bibliography, pp. 143–52.

Cranz, Annemarie. "Das aphoristische Element bei Matthias Claudius." Ph.D. diss., Freiburg, 1954. Treats a significant aspect of Claudius's style.

Delb, Heinrich. "Der launige Matthias Claudius." Ph.D. diss., Zurich, 1964. Discusses Claudius's humor as displayed in his life and work.

Diezel, Minna. Matthias Claudius: Sozialethischer Gehalt seiner Werke." Ph.D. diss., Vienna, 1948. Deals with Claudius's view of society and social relationships.

Fechner, Jörg-Ulrich. "Matthias Claudius und die Literatursoziologie?," *Geist und Zeichen: Festschrift für Arthur Henkel zu seinem 60. Geburtstag.* Edited by Herbert Anton, Bernhard Gajek, and Peter Pfaff. Heidelberg: Winter, 1977, pp. 57–74. Inquires into the possibility of a literary-sociological interpretation of Claudius's works.

Friedländer, Max. *Das deutsche Lied im 18. Jahrhundert: Quellen und Studien.* 2 vols. Stuttgart & Berlin: Cotta, 1902, 2:244–59.

Goedeke, Karl. *Grundriß zur Geschichte der deutschen Dichtung aus den Quellen.* 3d ed. Dresden: L. Ehlermann, 1916, 4:1, 973–83. Lists the older Claudius literature.

Görisch, Reinhold. *Matthias Claudius und der Sturm und Drang: Ein Abgrenzungsversuch.* Frankfurt am Main: Peter Lang, 1981. The first study by a theologian since Loofs's monograph to discuss in detail Claudius's religion and its relationship to the times, primarily to the *Sturm und Drang.* A significant work.

Herbst, Wilhelm. *Matthias Claudius der Wandsbecker Bote: ein deutsches Stillleben.* 3d ed. Gotha: Perthes, 1863. Still one of the major biographies, stressing the religious aspect of the life and work. This edition is the lengthiest and the last with annotations. The 4th, published in 1878, represents the author's final word and is the only one with an index.

Jones, G. L. "The Worldly Christian: Matthias Claudius as a Critic of His Time." *Modern Language Review* 71 (1976): 827–37. One of the few studies in English. Should be read critically.

König, Burghard. *Matthias Claudius: Die literarischen Beziehungen im Leben und Werk.* Bonn: Bouvier, 1976. One of the first serious literary studies of Claudius's prose. Contains mistakes, but is required reading.

Kraft, Werner. "Matthias Claudius und die Existenz." In his *Augenblicke der Dichtung: Kritische Betrachtungen.* Munich: Kösel, 1964, pp. 81–120. One of the few treatments of Claudius's pessimism. While valuable for that reason, it falls into the opposite extreme from the traditional view.

Kranefuß, Annelen. *Die Gedichte des Wandsbecker Boten.* Göttingen: Vandenhoeck & Ruprecht, 1973. Currently the most comprehensive and best study of Claudius's poetry.

Loofs, Friedrich. *Matthias Claudius in kirchengeschichtlicher Beleuchtung: Eine Untersuchung über Claudius' religiöse Stellung und Altersentwicklung.* Gotha: Perthes, 1915. An important study by a theologian of Claudius's relationship to the religious and philosophical currents of his time. It dispels the myth of a basic change in his position.

Mönckeberg, Carl. *Matthias Claudius: Ein Beitrag zur Kirchen-und Litterar-Geschichte seiner Zeit.* Hamburg: Nolte, 1869. Less useful than the other major biographies, but especially informative regarding the years of the Napoleonic Wars.

Naumann, Ferdinand. *Matthias Claudius und das Volkslied.* Ph.D. diss., Greifswald: Adler, 1914. An older but still useful study of Claudius's usage of folk-song tradition.

Nielsen, Ingeborg. "Matthias Claudius als Feuilletonist." Ph.D. diss., Freiburg, 1944. Investigates the influence of journalism, especially the feuilleton, on Claudius's literary style.

Petersen, Richard. *Matthias Claudius og Hans Vennekreds.* Copenhagen: Schønberg, 1884. A lengthy, relatively unknown work which concentrates chiefly on Claudius's friendships with the literary figures of the time and thus complements the major biographies with broader background material.

Pfeiffer, Johannes. *Matthias Claudius der Wandsbecker Bote: Eine Einführung in den Sinn seines Schaffens.* Dessau and Leipzig: Karl Rauch, 1940. Pfeiffer is one of the major commentators on Claudius, stressing the work as a literary expression of religion. This book contains most of the views and insights found in the author's many studies of Claudius.

Redlich, Carl. *Die poetischen Beiträge zum Wandsbecker Bothen, gesammelt und ihren Verfassern zugewiesen.* Hamburg: Meissner, 1871. A yeoman piece of work, which ascribes the lyrical contributions to *Der Wandsbecker Bote* to their authors as far as possible.

Roedl, Urban. *Matthias Claudius: Sein Weg und Seine Welt.* 3d. ed. Hamburg: Wittig, 1969. Another of the major comprehensive treatments of the life and work, balancing emphases on religion and literature.

Rowland, Herbert. "Matthias Claudius's *Paul Erdmanns Fest* and the Utopian Tradition." *Seminar* 18 (1982):14–26. The article treats the major prose expression of Claudius's view of society and politics within the utopian literary tradition. It also emphasizes Claudius's characteristic handling of the prose narrative.

———. "Matthias Claudius and Wieland." In: *Christoph Martin Wieland 1733–1813: North American Scholarly Contributions on the Occasion of the 250th Anniversary of His Birth.* To be published by Max Niemeyer Verlag in Tübingen in 1983. A study of the problematic relationship between the two authors.

Schmidt-Rohr, Christel. "Das Zeitungsschaffen des Matthias Claudius als formende Kraft in seinem Leben und Werk." Ph.D. diss., Heidelberg, 1944. Another discussion of the influence of journalistic form on Claudius's literary style.

Siebke, Rolf. "Arthur Schopenhauer und Matthias Claudius." *Schopenhauer-Jahrbuch* 51 (1970):22–31. A study of Claudius's reception by a major German philosopher.

Sommer, J. Carl Ernst. *Studien zu den Gedichten des Wandsbecker Boten.* Frankfurt am Main: Diesterweg, 1935; rpt. Hildesheim: Gerstenberg, 1973. A very useful study of the poetry, emphasizing literary technique.

Stammler, Wolfgang. *Matthias Claudius der Wandsbecker Bothe: Ein Beitrag zur deutschen Literatur- und Geistesgeschichte.* Halle: Waisenhaus, 1915. The major comprehensive study of the life and work from a primarily literary standpoint.

Stolpe, Albert. "Das Todesproblem in Matthias Claudius' Werken und Briefen." Ph.D. diss., Kiel, 1950. A discussion of a central experience and theme in Claudius's life and work.

Zimmermann, Rolf Christian. "Matthias Claudius." In: *Deutsche Dichter des 18. Jahrhunderts: Ihr Leben und Werk.* Edited by Benno von Wiese. Berlin: Erich Schmidt, 1977. Valuable largely as an example of the negative response to Claudius.

Index